Glimpses of God

Glimpses of God

edited by
Dan Cohn-Sherbok

Duckworth

First published in 1994 by
Gerald Duckworth & Co. Ltd.
The Old Piano Factory
48 Hoxton Square, London N1 6PB
Tel: 071 729 5986
Fax: 071 729 0015

A catalogue record for this book is available from the British Library

ISBN 0 7156 2608 6

Typeset by Ray Davies
Printed in Great Britain by
Redwood Books Trowbridge

Contents

Foreword

The Most Rev. Desmond Tutu, Archbishop of Cape Town

There is a Jewish story from the concentration camps. A Nazi guard used to torment one of his Jewish charges who one day was made to clean out the filthy toilets. Gloatingly the guard looked down on his victim and taunted him with, 'Where is your God now?' The little Jew replied quietly, 'He is right here with me in the muck.' The God whom some of us worship is the God who is found in the fiery furnace, not giving good advice from a safe distance about the protective qualities of asbestos. He is right there as Immanuel, God with us – identifying with the lost, the poor, the voiceless, those without much influence, those whom Jesus was to call 'the least of my brethren'. Our God vouchsafes theophanies in the unspectacular, the ordinary, the humdrum, for He is the immanent one 'in whom we live and move and have our being'.

But that is only one aspect of the splendour of His being, for this God is also the one who is high and lifted up, whose train fills the temple and all His creatures are overwhelmed with awe as they veil their sight before His all-consuming holiness, which makes a Gerontius cry out in anguished tones, in Elgar's *Dream of Gerontius*, 'Take me away' – for the frail creature is but a man of unclean lips, dwelling among people of unclean lips, since God is also the transcendent, all holy, omnipotent, omniscient one and we must repent in dust and ashes when we must speak in His name.

A dispirited Elijah went to Mount Horeb hoping for a reassuring encounter with God. And he got it, but not in the spectacular conventional ways he had come to expect. God was not in the fire, not in the earthquake, nor in the wind – traditional revelations of the Divine. This time God was in the still small voice. It seems that a particular point was being made emphatically. That God is not bound to reveal Himself only in the spectacular, the abnormal, the unusual, but can and does reveal Himself also in the usual, the commonplace. And so our God can reveal Himself in a baby in a manger, in bread and wine, in a glorious sunset, and a beautiful Beethoven symphony as in the stillness of mystical contemplation. The whole of His creation can be as transparent as a silken veil to show forth the wonders of its Creator.

But even more wonderfully, God is encountered not just in the beautiful and attractive, but may be found in the ugly, the repellent – even in the evil and atrocious, as with a young man dying an excruciating death on a Cross. Ultimately there is nowhere where God is not. The fetid squalor of the slum can be as holy ground as the most beautiful sanctuary.

Doesn't the psalmist exult in the wonder of God's omnipresence in these words:

> Whither shall I go from thy Spirit?
> or wither shall I flee from thy presence?
> If I ascend to heaven, thou art there!
> If I make my bed in Sheol, thou art there!
> If I take the wings of the morning and dwell in the
> uttermost parts of the sea,
> even there thy hand shall lead me, and thy right hand
> shall hold me.
> If I say, 'Let only darkness cover me, and the light about
> me by night',
> even the darkness is not dark to thee, the night is bright
> as the day;
> for darkness is as light with thee.
>
> Psalm 139:7-12

The present anthology records the wide range of possibilities for the encounter with God.

Contributors

PROFESSOR SIR NORMAN ANDERSON is Emeritus Professor of Oriental Laws and was Director of the Institute of Advanced Legal Studies in the University of London

THE RT. REV. MICHAEL BALL is Bishop of Truro

THE RT. REV. LORD BLANCH was formerly Archbishop of York

THE RT. HON. SIR RHODES BOYSON, PC is Conservative MP for Brent North

THE REV. MARCUS BRAYBROOKE was formerly Executive Director of the Council of Christians and Jews

THE VERY REV. WESLEY CARR is Dean of Bristol

DAME BARBARA CARTLAND is a best-selling novelist and writer

THE RT. REV. LORD COGGAN was formerly Archbishop of Canterbury

BARONESS COX is an educationalist and is active in medical aid in Poland

THE REV. DON CUPITT is University Lecturer in Divinity at Cambridge

TAM DALYELL is Labour MP for Linlithgow

SISTER FRANCIS DOMINICA is a member and was formerly Superior of the Society of All Saints, Oxford

PROFESSOR ARTHUR ELLISON is Emeritus Professor of Electrical and Electronic Engineering in the City University, London

AUDREY EYTON is a best-selling author

THE REV. PROFESSOR ROBIN GILL is Michael Ramsey Professor of Modern Theology in the University of Kent

LORD GRIMOND was leader of the Liberal Party from 1956 to 1967. He died in 1993.

THE RT. REV. ROBERT HARDY is Bishop of Lincoln

TED HARRISON is a broadcaster and writer

THE REV. CHRISTOPHER HILL is a Residentiary Canon of St Paul's

THE REV. PROFESSOR LESLIE HOULDEN is Professor of Theology at King's College, London

THE REV. CANON ERIC JAMES is Director of Christian Action

SIR LARRY LAMB was formerly Editor of the *Sun* and the *Daily Express*

SIR JOHN LAWRENCE, Bt. is a writer and expert on Christianity in Russia

THE VERY REV. CHRISTOPHER LEWIS is Dean of St Albans

THE REV. PROFESSOR ANDREW LINZEY is Special Professor at the University of Nottingham and IFAW Senior Research Fellow of Mansfield College, Oxford

THE REV. PROFESSOR DAVID MARTIN is Emeritus Professor of Sociology at the London School of Economics

THE VERY REV. MICHAEL MAYNE is Dean of Westminster

PETER MULLEN is a journalist and writer

RABBI JULIA NEUBERGER is a writer and broadcaster

THE REV. DR EDWARD NORMAN is Dean of Christ Church College, Canterbury

THE REV. CANON ANTHONY PHILLIPS is Headmaster of King's School, Canterbury

THE REV. CANON PETER PILKINGTON was High Master of St Paul's School and is now Chairman of the Broadcasting Complaints Commission

THE REV. PROFESSOR JOHN POLKINGHORNE is President of Queens' College, Cambridge

THE REV. PROFESSOR CHRISTOPHER ROWLAND is Dean Ireland's Professor of the Exegesis of Holy Scripture at Oxford

DAME CICELY SAUNDERS is Chairman of St Christopher's Hospice

PROFESSOR ERICH SEGAL is a classical scholar and best-selling novelist

THE VERY REV. JOHN SIMPSON is Dean of Canterbury

THE REV. NICHOLAS STACEY was formerly Director of Kent Social Services

SIR SIGMUND STERNBERG is Chairman of the Council of Christians and Jews

THE RT. REV. MICHAEL TURNBULL is Bishop of Rochester

THE REV. DR JOHN VINCENT is Superintendent of Sheffield Inner City Ecumenical Mission and Director of the Urban Theology Unit in Sheffield

THE VERY REV. ALAN WEBSTER was formerly Dean of St Paul's

MRS MARY WHITEHOUSE is President of the National Viewers' and Listeners' Association

Introduction

Rabbi Professor Dan Cohn-Sherbok

In the twentieth century religious experience has often been regarded with suspicion – it is frequently perceived as hallucinatory in character or the result of an overactive spiritual enthusiasm. In the past this was not the case. From the Biblical period to the time of the Enlightenment believers were convinced of the validity of their experiences. However, in modern times the growth of science has given rise to widespread suspicion and even hostility towards religion. The purpose of this collection is to testify to the persistence of spiritual encounter and explore its nature.

Contributors to this book – distinguished clergymen and women, theologians, writers and politicians – were asked to discuss their own personal glimpses of God and reflect on the nature of such experience. As can be seen, these responses and meditations embrace a wide variety of viewpoints; this is highlighted by the fact that various terms are used to designate divine reality. Yet in their different ways these testimonies bear witness to the continuing experience of God in contemporary society.

The book begins with a preface by Archbishop Desmond Tutu in which he emphasises that God manifests himself in numerous ways, from his magnificent presence in the ancient Temple in Jerusalem to the still small voice revealed to Elijah on Mt Horeb. God, he stresses, reveals himself in the spectacular, as well as in the commonplace and even in what is repellent.

The book continues in Part I with a series of depictions of moments of revelation. The writer Audrey Eyton explains that, at the time of the death of her first child, she experienced tangible evidence of the presence of God. In this tragedy, she felt supported and came to see things from a heavenly viewpoint. Paradoxically through this trauma, she even felt joyful – yet this divine presence disappeared as quickly as it had arrived. In the years that followed, such an overwhelming perception of God did not recur. None the less she has continued to be sustained by small fragments of divine experience.

In the next essay the former editor, Sir Larry Lamb, emphasises that, although he does not claim to have had an experience of God, he did feel the overwhelming presence of something when he underwent a serious heart operation. At this time he had the impression that he had left his body, hovered above it, and then moved into a long, dark tunnel at the end of which a faint glow emerged which was transformed into a burning globe of incandescence inside which appeared a half-formed bearded figure with his arms outstretched. A similar experience took place during a second operation. Uncertain how to interpret these near-death experiences, he remains sceptical of their spiritual significance. However, he is persuaded that the next time he travels down this dark tunnel he may well be transported home to God, or alternatively to oblivion.

Unlike Sir Larry Lamb, the Anglican theologian Professor Andrew Linzey has always been convinced of God's presence in the world. For Linzey God is revealed in nature, and most particularly in the animal world. It is in creation, he believes, that we are guided into an awareness of the sacredness of all creatures. To feel their suffering, he maintains, is divine grace. For this reason he has committed himself to combating the exploitation of animals in the modern world.

For the Rt. Rev. Robert Hardy, Bishop of Lincoln, it was during National Service that he had an overwhelming experience of God while attending Evensong in Hereford Cathedral. He stresses that there was nothing dramatic about this encounter: there was no voice, command, or vision. Rather, a definite presence, a disclosure, a reassurance – an almost tangible experience – occurred which has remained vivid and fervent. When he came out of the Cathedral, he knew that God was real. Even though he has subsequently attended services repeatedly, such an experience has never been repeated.

For Dame Cicely Saunders, Chairman of St Christopher's Hospice, the writings of C.S. Lewis, William Temple and Dorothy Sayers led her to search for the Divine. Through a series of losses, she perceived God's guidance; it was, she writes, like suddenly feeling the wind at one's back instead of battling against it all the time. Such a gift of awareness opened ways to meet the needs of other people; for Dame Cicely, this experience resulted in her dedication to the Hospice movement.

An experience of a different order is depicted in the novelist Dame Barbara Cartland's account of an event that took place after the death of her husband. A week after his funeral the maid asked her if she had noticed the scent of carnations outside her husband's dressing-room. Astonished by this fragrance, she consulted a medium about its significance; after this encounter, she perceived its meaning. Every year she and her husband went to Paris for a 'second honeymoon'. There he bought her bunches of carnations before they went to

Church. For Dame Barbara, the fragrance she perceived at home was the means by which her husband was communicating to her that there is life after death.

The politician Tam Dalyell gives a very different account of his experience of the Divine. It is in nature, he explains, that he most clearly apprehends God's presence. In particular, it is in the tropical rain forest that he has most clearly encountered God's presence. The rain forest, he writes, is essential to the survival of life, and we in the developed world have a sacred responsibility for its existence. Experiencing the Divine thus imposes obligations on all of us.

The former Archbishop of Canterbury, Donald Coggan, emphasises that God is manifest in many places. Yet for him the nearest he came to hearing a voice from heaven was during the war. Travelling to a new post in London, he was on a train which rolled through the blackout; there he heard the words: 'You have not chosen me, I have chosen you and ordained you.' That night these words were a benediction and an assurance.

Like other writers, Sister Francis Dominica of the All Saints Convent writes that she is able to find God in nature. Yet she stresses that it is most particularly in human suffering that she perceives God's indwelling. 'He had the face of a woman,' she writes, 'her eyes red and stained with crying, barely talking with grief. Three days ago her children had been buried.' For Sister Francis it is in such tragedy – where pain and anguish are found – that she most clearly catches a glimpse of God's presence.

Focusing on his background in a non-conformist family in Lancashire, Sir Rhodes Boyson MP describes how at one stage a large lump appeared in his mother's breast. After praying, the lump disappeared – she had no doubt that this was the action of the Almighty. In this religious environment Sir Rhodes felt God's presence. He goes on to describe how he himself had an overpowering religious experience when faced by a particular problem. Refusing to go to Church, he stayed at home to pray. After half an hour, his mind cleared as if in a blinding flash. Later in life, he recounts, his divergence from the Labour Party was motivated in part by religious convictions.

The writer Peter Mullen's contribution is drawn from an autobiographical novel in which he describes how he discovered God in a local church. Here he discovered 'religion without condemnation; religion with real music; religion that was not a denial of colour and light'. For him such an experience was incredible, and he concludes by depicting a scene in which he resisted the urge to tell an unhappy person that going to church would be good for her.

In another autobiographical essay, Professor David Martin gives an account of several religious experiences. The first took place when he was nine. At the end of *Children's Hour*, the Hallelujah Chorus was played. As the trumpet sounded, he was overcome with discomfort and wanted to rush out in a flood of tears. Later, as a conscript, he took a bus to Ludlow which ended with an experience of religious elation. Another experience of overwhelming impact occurred in a Methodist Church in Poole, and the final divine disclosure came on a plane from Washington to London.

The broadcaster and writer, Rabbi Julia Neuberger, finds God in pain and suffering. Over the years she has found the Divine in the goodness of those who care for the dying and in the acceptance of those who die. 'This sense of the divine presence,' she writes, 'is round about me, cradling me, comforting me in the bleak moments, making it tolerable to watch the intolerable.'

In Part II contributors discuss the experience of divine reality in the context of their personal histories. Canon Anthony Phillips, Headmaster of King's School, Canterbury, explains that as a youth it was in a Cornish village church and the surrounding countryside that he felt the presence of God. Later there was no overwhelming event which led to his ordination as an Anglican priest, but rather a sense of wholeness that can only be attained by an abandonment of all that has been before.

For the writer Sir John Lawrence, an encounter with Baron von Huegel in Kensington Gardens at the age of four initiated his religious quest. His whole early childhood, he recounts, was filled with the glory of God. Subsequently there was a slow erosion of faith; yet after reading St Mark's Gospel he became convinced that Christianity was true, and this has led to a spiritual journey in which prayer plays an important role.

The Anglican priest, Nicholas Stacey, writes that he first experienced the Divine most vividly through the death and destruction that he saw at Hiroshima. When he arrived, two months after the bomb had been dropped, the city stank of death and decay. It was here that he felt the call of God to be in the front line against human evil. 'The place then for me,' he wrote, 'was not the bridge of a ship but the pulpit of the Church.'

For Baroness Cox an experience of God's presence has been manifest through her work with the impoverished. In particular her efforts to bring aid to Eastern Europe have revealed to her the depth of courage of those facing oppression and death. In her depiction of those she met she provides an insight into their faith in adversity, hope in tragedy, and love through persecution. In their lives she witnessed the power of a loving God whose ways are not those of this world.

The Anglican priest, Marcus Braybrooke, has similarly found God manifest among those in foreign lands. At the Satcitananda ashram in South India he experienced God's presence in the celebration of the Eucharist which incorporated various aspects of Hindu Temple ritual. Such an experience of limitless divine love was not new – he had sensed God's presence in the desert of Sinai and the outback of Australia. Yet what was different was that beside the sea the presence of mystery in nature and the revelation of Jesus of infinite love were linked.

By contrast Professor Sir Norman Anderson emphasises that his experience of God comes through the Bible rather than any direct revelation. The lynchpin of his faith, he explains, is the evidence for the resurrection of Jesus Christ from the dead as recorded in Scripture. Through his experiences in the Middle East and in England his faith in Christ was strengthened – even through times of pain and suffering.

The Jewish businessman, Sir Sigmund Sternberg, stresses that his orthodox background provided the basis for belief in God. Later, the war years provided ample opportunities to turn to God. Yet Sir Sigmund's response to the events of the Nazi period was to dedicate himself to building a better world through inter-religious dialogue. Even if such activity is not an experience of the Divine, such commitment is, he believes, a way of doing God's will.

For Lord Blanch his early years provided a glimpse of the Divine. Later, serving in the RAF, this experience of God deepened when he read the Gospels seriously for the first time. Subsequently, he relates, he was inspired by a book, *Midnight Hour*, which presented the starkness of the choice between what life might offer and what Christ demands. Throughout a busy life as a country parson, a theological teacher, Bishop of Liverpool, and Archbishop of York, he has attempted to respond to the sense of God's presence amidst the ordinary concerns of everyday experience.

The Dean of Canterbury, John Simpson, emphasises that experiencing God is not susceptible to proof – it is a matter of faith. For Christians, worship has provided the focus of such encounter. Hence it is through acts of worship, poetry, music, silence, colour and movement that an awareness of God can be found. The Christian Eucharist in particular reveals God's saving action through Christ. As he writes: 'What we do with bread and wine takes us to the heart of God and his torn world, and at the same time to his victory and re-creation of mankind and the world in glory.'

By contrast the Jewish novelist and classical scholar, Erich Segal, portrays an experience of the Divine through a passage from his recent novel, *Acts of Faith*. In this work, he depicts an act of exorcism among the Hasidim – through contact with the demonic realm, those involved are able to gain a glimpse of the supernatural.

The Dean of Bristol, Wesley Carr, stresses that religious experience is indirect in character – it consistently moves to and through the unknown. Using the symbolism of Cathedral architecture, he explores the transcendent and immanent nature of divine disclosure. 'Experiencing the Divine for me,' he states, 'is inevitably informed by the basic ambiguity of cathedrals and churches.'

Approaching this topic from a different standpoint, the liberal politician Lord Grimond, who died recently, stresses that he has had no personal experience of the Divine – his life had not been illuminated by glimpses of heaven. None the less, his experience of life led him to believe in the existence of non-material value. For Lord Grimond the existence of goodness in the moral sphere and elsewhere is a manifestation of divine presence.

The scientist and theologian, the Rev. Professor John Polkinghorne, argues that the intellectual joy that scientists feel at the beautiful patterns of the physical world is an experience of the Divine. Whether they recognise such an experience or not, they are able to enter into the thoughts of the Creator. Yet this is only one dimension of divine experience. For Polkinghorne, worship provides a framework for encountering God as a person. The daily routine of prayer and the weekly gathering with other Christians for the celebration of the Eucharist provides him with a sustaining basis for his religious life.

The Very Rev. Christopher Lewis stresses that God is present in certain special places and on particular occasions. For him it is often when taking strenuous exercise in striking surroundings that he has an experience of the Divine. Describing his participation in the London Marathon, he writes that the key experience 'was that of padding along with others for mile after mile, united by a common purpose and encouraged by thousands of people who were supporting everyone indiscriminately ... in me there was the sense that this is how things are meant to be: the unity of people, the rhythm of life, the body and the spirit working in unison.'

Professor Leslie Houlden traces his experience of the divine presence to an event that took place when he was serving as a soldier in northern Germany in 1948. There he heard a sermon which altered the course of his life. It was, he writes, 'the day of no return'. This was not an end but a new beginning in the development of his spiritual journey.

For Canon Christopher Hill of St Paul's Cathedral the way of unknowing is an authentic path to the Divine. In addition, for him the sacraments provide a means of experiencing God. Yet he notes that, however real the experience of God is through the sacramental, it is never direct – it is mediated through human experience. Thus, although God does reveal himself to humanity, his presence remains a mystery which we can only perceive through a glass darkly.

Writing from a different perspective, the Methodist theologian, Dr John Vincent, emphasises that experience of the Divine takes place when people put themselves in a position of discipleship. According to Vincent, in Christianity such discipleship is primarily about personal loyalty rather than abstract ideas, values, spirituality or systems. This means that following Christ involves a commitment to bring about the kingdom of God on earth. For Vincent this can only be accomplished by standing alongside those who are disadvantaged in society.

For the Very Rev. Alan Webster reflecting on Julian of Norwich led to an experience of the Divine. Serving as Dean in Julian's city encouraged him to share her experience that the Divine Spirit loves humanity. Opening the Close to those in need, he came to perceive God's presence among the desolate. Later in the Cathedral, he experienced the Divine at a celebration of Julian. 'I felt a strange movement of the spirit as Christians rose above the barriers which had barred them from sharing Communion or accepting the leadership of women ... perhaps because Julian had insisted that we should consider the motherhood of God and even Christ as our mother as well as our brother, I experienced at the Cathedral the Divine joy, as I had never experienced it before.'

Reflecting over eighty-one years, Mary Whitehouse states that she perceived God in unexpected places. In particular she gives an account of her struggle with malaria; although incapacitated at the time, she was taken on as a part-time senior mistress in a local school. It was out of this experience that she embarked on advocacy of moral standards in the media. For her, the creation of the National Viewers' and Listeners' Association was a response to what she conceived as God's will.

The former High Master of St Paul's School, Canon Peter Pilkington, also describes the evolution of his religious conviction. At first as a small boy he polished the mahogany and crude mosaics in a Primitive Methodist Church in the Durham mining village where he lived. Eventually he began to experience a mystery and depth to existence which could not be contained within the northern creed of hard work. As time passed, he became increasingly committed to Christianity, particularly working with the Universities Mission to Central Africa. Here, he explains, he experienced the Divine in a way that has never left him.

In Part III, Reflections on Religious Experience, the theologian Dr Edward Norman discusses the nature of religious experience in modern society. In the past, he notes, religion was generally a collective experience; however, in contemporary society, a large number of people report having had some sense of a divine presence. Yet, he maintains, these experiences have a close relationship to cultural expectations. The human imagination has an enormous capacity for self-fulfilment. In this light he proposes a return to religion as a matter of allegiance rather than feelings.

The Rt. Rev. Michael Turnbull, Bishop of Rochester, similarly emphasises that experience of the Divine is dangerous if it relies solely on individual response. Yet, at the other extreme, it is possible to be too analytical about our experiences. What is thus required is an approach which draws together the subjective and objective into a harmonious whole. In this quest, the experience of the Divine is never a completion – rather it is a journey of discovery.

For the Rt. Rev. Michael Ball, Bishop of Truro, the major wonder in that divine encounter we call 'prayer' is the humility of God. Here he writes that, in God's lowliness, he allows the things of creation to express prayerful intimacy. 'In the divine human encounter in prayer,' he writes, 'it is the humility of God that overwhelms us. For in that divine human encounter is, in the end, an encounter, a secret swapping within the Holy Trinity itself.'

According to Professor Christopher Rowland, the experience of divine reality occurs in ordinary everyday contexts. Citing Biblical examples, he emphasises that religious experience is not a warm feeling within, but rather is directly related to acts of righteousness: one meets in the poor, the outcast and the vulnerable none other than the representation of the Judge of the world.

For Eric James, being a biographer has led to a recognition that God calls particular individuals to a life of dedicated work. Reflecting on his biography of Archbishop Trevor Huddleston, he states that in writing his biography he has been able to experience the Divine.

Approaching divine experience from another perspective, the Dean of Westminster stresses that all of creation is a sacrament of God's presence; every human being is made in God's image and thus is a reflection of the Divine. Surveying various writings about Epiphanies, he maintains that God encourages us to use the material world as a means of finding him. Yet ultimately it is Christ who discloses God most fully.

According to Professor Robin Gill, goodness beyond self-interest offers clues about the experience of the Divine. In this view, acts of altruism abound in contemporary society; they point to a loving God who wishes his creatures to act in accord with his nature. Thus he argues that there is a strong connection between morality and faith, and in this sense the Divine can be experienced in our daily lives.

In Professor Arthur Ellison's view, experiencing the Divine is a personal activity, usually expressed in symbolic or archetypal form. In all the world's religions, he continues, mystical experience is characteristic of such encounter. For Ellison, the near-death experience is in some respects similar to such mystical activity. In his presentation, he urges readers to adopt a new paradigm of human experience and reject the common scientific view that human beings are simply biochemical machines.

In the opinion of the broadcaster Ted Harrison, it is important for religious journalists to adopt a detached stance. In his years as a religious correspondent he has been keen to observe how other people claim to be experiencing the Divine and how they react to what they believe God expects of them. All that a reporter on religious affairs can do is to say to both believers and non-believers alike that the search for evidence of God at work in the world is a serious matter.

This collection of reflections about the nature of religious experience concludes with a cautionary note by the Rev. Don Cupitt. It is important to remember, he stresses, that the experience of a divine reality is shaped by one's own personal background. Although people want to believe that their experience of the Divine is given from above, such experiences cannot be separated from the individual history of the believer. According to Cupitt, our religious experiences are the products of our own cultural and intellectual history.

This book thus provides a fascinating insight into what it means to be touched by the Divine today. Given the universal nature of religious experience, it was considered appropriate to donate the royalties to Oxfam, whose purpose is to help the needy throughout the world.

Part I

Moments of Revelation

1

Audrey Eyton

The loss of a small baby, whom one has never even held, cannot compare in depth of sorrow with the loss of an only son to whom one has been totally devoted for twenty-four years. The ten-day life of my first son, Richard, now seems like a sad but passing incident in my life. Matthew, my second son, who died on April 18, 1991, aged twenty-four, *was* my life. With him also passed away all my future hopes of happiness on this earth.

Yet it was at the time of the birth and death of Richard, twenty-seven years ago, that I experienced my most 'tangible' – I use this for lack of a better word – evidence of the presence of God. I had always associated this experience with his death, but now, forced to recall more precisely in order to write it down, I realise that it occurred mainly during his short lifetime.

I was happy and unsuspecting when I woke up in hospital the morning after Richard's birth. It was only when screens were pulled around my bed and I was told that Sister would like to see me that I began to realise that all was not well.

The full severity of this baby's physical defects were only revealed little by little over a number of days. But it quickly became apparent that he would never walk. It was with this realisation that what I have later come to think of as the Holy Spirit seemed to join me.

How to describe this experience is the problem and probably the reason why many people are shy of explaining their personal glimpses of God. Putting it into words is like trying to grab handfuls of a cloud from a mountain top.

The best I can do is to say that I felt supported, lifted up, and viewed everything and everyone in a kinder, wiser, stronger and quite different way. For a short time I seemed to see things from a heavenly rather than an earthly viewpoint. I even seem to recall glimpses of joy. I was a better person than I have been before or since. A different person. Perhaps, I have often thought, I became for a while the kind of person I hope to become in another world.

Friends said that I was 'wonderful'. Perhaps I was. But only because I had this strong sense of being helped and lifted into a new dimension. At the same time I retained an earthly realism. When it was eventually revealed that Richard had such tissue-thin bones that he would never leave a bed I wished devoutly that he would die and was deeply relieved when he did so.

The 'presence' left as suddenly as it had arrived, about two days after he died, and I remember this moment quite clearly. One tiny note of discord arose as my husband and I drove home after a visit to friends, and immediately I was back on my own earthly level and remained so. Comforted though. I have never made a fuss about the loss of that child; many of my dearest friends of later years have not even known of his life and death. I felt fortunate to have been helped, fortunate that both the baby and I were spared further suffering, and even more fortunate when a seemingly healthy son was born to me two years later. To have grieved would have seemed ungrateful.

The experience didn't have any dramatic and instant effect on my faith. Brought up by parents who believed in God, it seemed natural for me to do so. However, there have been long periods of my life when God has been pushed to the back of my mind and in the same way that 'glimpse of God' was pushed to the back of my mind – still there but stored away in the least accessible place under the great pile of current clutter of everyday life and concerns.

When my 'perfect' child, Matthew, reached the age of thirteen it began to become evident that all was not well with him either. Matthew was a unique character, aglow with wit, warmth, intelligence and love, but the first signs of a mysterious illness that was later to be labelled Obsessive Compulsive Disorder were beginning to torment him. For ten years he valiantly struggled with what has been described as the most agonising of all illnesses of the mind, in its most severe form. Such was his courage and spirit that many who knew him did not even suspect that anything ailed him.

His life was a struggle to find God and make sense of pain, theology his natural choice of subject when he went to university, and most of all, like so many people, he longed for proof.

'God doesn't pop up wearing a long white beard with GOD written across it,' I used to joke, but nevertheless, at his frequent request, I would tell him again about what we called 'my experience with the baby'.

That experience came to the forefront of my mind again in 1989 when Matthew and I sat holding my mother's hand as she died gently in perfect peace and faith. I half hoped it would be repeated, but no, there was no need for such support during this natural and gentle passing.

As Matthew struggled to find God, during his late teens and early twenties, my own faith gradually deepened. 'Pray to YOUR God for me, won't you?' he always asked (during his off-God periods) as I set off to attend services at Canterbury Cathedral. I did, and for a time, while he was studying for his degree at King's College London, we both believed he was getting better. It was only after he achieved his goals, an excellent degree and the offer of a post-graduate place at Cambridge, that he began to spiral downwards at a terrifying rate during a year off to complete his treatment.

More and more the agonising fantasies caused by this dreadful illness took over his mind. I prayed, but in a different way, as hope slipped away. On several occasions I asked: 'If there is to be agony let it be mine, not his.' That prayer was to be answered, but in a way I had never envisaged, when I opened Matthew's bedroom door on April 18 and found him dead.

Strangely, it was during the stunned and terrible hours and days after Matthew's death that I became most aware of the help I had been given during the lifetime of my first baby. Not because the same experience recurred, but because it did not. At some level of my mind the memory was still so vivid that I expected the same intervention and was deeply aware of its lack. 'God doesn't seem to be here,' I told the kind Canon, who came from the Cathedral to sit with me.

In the days, weeks and months that followed I became aware of God's help in a different way and came to understand the meaning of the words 'God doesn't spare us from suffering, but he shares it with us', written in a letter from my son's school chaplain. Friends were overwhelmingly kind. Of course they were. But complete strangers too seemed to sense and respond to my deepest moments of need. The lovely young woman who was sitting in the Cathedral Memorial garden when I first went alone to stand by Matthew's unmarked grave, the waiter in a Brighton restaurant who seemed to sense a deep moment of anguish. ...

God doesn't make it easy but he does make it endurable. I have learned to trust to his intervention when I sink below a certain depth of suffering. But not intervention by the seemingly supernatural, rather by the natural order of good and loving things ... a phone call, a letter, a visit, a sunny sky, the goodness and love of people.

Knowing my greater strength in my later years God has, this time, supported me in a different way. Or so it seems to me. I have always believed that he prefers, if possible, not to perform miracles.

Did the Holy Spirit really lift me up and sustain me for those ten days so long ago? Was it, perhaps, a chemical reaction resulting from profound shock? If so, why not the same reaction after the far, far greater shock and loss of Matthew's death?

All I have experienced and experience now is capable of earthly explanation – chemical reaction to shock, the kindness of friends, even an aura of grief that can be sensed by strangers. And yet, behind it all, I sense God, not with an unwavering faith, but with one which always returns.

I worry about my child, one does not cease to worry about a beloved child because he is dead. Where is he, how is he, what is he, and will we be together again? I experience, from time to time, all the intense need for proof that he experienced in his profound pain. 'Sorry,' I find myself saying to friends, when tears suddenly fill my eyes at the most unexpected and inconvenient moments. 'Sorry,' Matthew used to say, over and over again, feeling guilt when the torment of his illness overwhelmed the brilliant logic of his mind, aware that he suffered alone in a totally uncomprehending world. 'Sorry' was the last word he ever wrote. In so many ways I now experience so many of the emotions that he felt. Some prayers, but only the right prayers, I suspect, are answered.

What sustains and supports me is not the memory of just one glimpse of God, but a whole accumulation of fragments of such experiences during fifty-six years. 'Gut-feel' action or reaction, a psychiatrist friend once explained, is not an unscientific leap in the dark but the result of thousands of little fragments of information which have been accumulated in the mind. Often they do not add up to a sentence which can be expressed verbally, but nevertheless send powerful messages which we are wise to heed. During my years in journalism I learned to trust and follow my gut-feel. Not until months later, when those fragments had assembled into a picture in the kaleidoscope of my mind, could I explain (or know) precisely why I had insisted on a certain course of action.

Archbishop Carey, interviewed during the week in which he was enthroned, which was also the week during which Matthew died, explained that on some occasions he has embarked on a course of action and only realised later that 'he had been called to do so'. Another way, it seemed to me, of expressing the same thing.

It is through a million microscopic glimpses rather than one supernatural experience that God most often chooses to reveal himself.

2

Sir Larry Lamb

I am a retired journalist. Primarily, though not exclusively, a 'pop' journalist. Academic I am not. My best friends would not claim that I had serious pretensions to intellectualism. What is more, I do not claim to have experienced the Divine. I am not even sure that I believe in the existence of a Divinity. *Any* Divinity. Whether or not it is one that shapes our ends. I have, however, 'died' twice. And dying is an experience, divine or not, which certainly gives one cause furiously to think. I will write briefly of those experiences. There is nothing particularly novel in them. Many people have been dragged back from the brink of death by agencies they knew not of, and for purposes they failed to understand. For many of them, myself included, the experiences were remarkably similar.

The significance of my own flirtations with death, if there is any significance at all, is simply that I experienced them *twice*, in much the same form. And that on each occasion I, a professional unbeliever, a prototype agnostic, if you like, felt overwhelmingly the presence of *something* outside my ability to comprehend.

Very early one morning, in the deep mid-winter of 1961, I was driving home to Wimbledon from a late, late shift at the *Daily Mirror.* I made a detour over Lambeth Bridge to take home a colleague whose flat was not far off my route.

At a darkened crossroads just north of the river, within spitting distance of the Westminster Hospital, I was 'in collision with' a truck, as the police say. My car, a strongly-built Wolseley 4/44, was virtually destroyed. My passengers, miraculously, were only slightly hurt. But I was smashed to bits.

I 'sustained', they told me afterwards, multiple injuries, including a cracked skull, broken ribs, one bit of which penetrated a lung, and, more importantly, a ruptured spleen.

If I had chosen to have a ruptured spleen I couldn't have chosen to have it in a better place. The Registrar at the Westminster, where I was taken, was something of an authority on spleens, and had written what was apparently, at that time, the definitive textbook on the subject.

At first, it was not apparent to the staff of the Westminster just why

I was hovering on the brink. The injuries they had identified were not, on the face of it, life-threatening. So twenty-four hours after I was admitted they embarked upon an exploratory operation, necessitating huge incisions, which has left me with a scar about twelve inches deep and all of eight inches wide. But they found the culprit, the spleen, which had been ruptured against the steering wheel, and took it out. I know exactly how they took it out. Because I saw them. Long before the operation was finished I had 'left' my body, and hovered above it. I was totally dispassionate about what was happening to me. I felt no pain, and no anxiety. I heard the conversation of the operating team quite clearly. And when it was over, I saw the surgeon turn to the anaesthetist with a shrug, a resigned gesture with open arms which said quite clearly: 'We have done all we can.' That, I think, was the point at which I left the land of the living, and moved into the long, dark tunnel.

Like others before me, I felt as though I was being swept along on a soft, warm wind, at first in complete darkness. Then, gradually, a faint glow emerged, a long, long way ahead. I wasn't thinking about anything in particular, but I did recall, with a flicker of amusement, the words of the man in the bed alongside me in the casualty ward to the patient on his other side, when my bed was being moved to a place behind the door the night before the operation. 'He won't last,' he said. 'They always move them there when they're going. So as not to disturb the rest of us, like, when they move them out, you see.' As this thought crossed my mind, the light at the end of the tunnel grew brighter and brighter. Suddenly it was a fierce, burning globe of incandescence, the height of a man. Fleetingly, I thought I saw a half-formed, bearded figure inside it with arms outstretched towards me. Then all was blackness again.

I do not now attach any importance to the figure. I was brought up a practising Christian, sang in the Church choir, taught in Sunday School. I thought it not too improbable, in retrospect, that I could have dredged up an image of Christ from the depths of a drugged imagination.

But I did not imagine the tunnel, or the light. Of that I am convinced.

I emerged from the blackness – many hours later, I was told – back in the ward in the bed behind the door. Two days later I was moved to the middle of the ward.

More than twenty years later, when I was Editor of the *Daily Express*, I had a heart attack in the office. I had read enough to know that overweight, middle-aged, heavy smokers in stressful occupations were quite likely to have heart attacks. And I identified the symptoms – searing chest pain, and a devastating numbness down one side – precisely.

While still conscious, I pressed hard on the buzzer, which brought my Deputy and my good friend Leith McGrandle rushing in from the office next door.

'I am having a heart attack, Leith,' I told him. 'Get the nurse. Tell her to ring Bart's. And tell her she will need oxygen.'

The reader will recall that my first near-death experience had been on the steps of the Westminster Hospital. With the luck of one born to be hanged I had my second within a three-minute drive of St Bartholomew's.

By the time the office medical staff had got me into a wheelchair and into a back-of-the-building goods lift, a fully-equipped ambulance from the hospital's cardiac unit was backing into the loading bay.

I 'left' my body as I was being 'stretchered' (as the football writers say) into the ambulance. And again, with an overwhelming sense of *déjà vu*, I hovered above myself, watching with some detachment the frantic struggle to keep me alive.

People seemed to be sticking a lot of things in me, often with tubes attached.

I recall with great clarity a handful of phrases:

'Quick, quick, he's going' was clear enough.

'Give me a line, a line. I must have another line' meant presumably that the paramedic concerned was anxious to find another way of pumping drugs into my bloodstream.

At that point, I left them, and found myself back in my old friend, the long, dark tunnel.

I will not bore the reader by recounting that experience all over again. It differed scarcely at all from the first time.

Again, I felt quite serene. This time, I think, I felt rather more strongly that I was dead or dying. But it didn't worry me. Indeed I almost felt, as the poet has it, 'half in love with easeful death'.

And there swam then into my mind, as they have often done since, the subsequent lines from 'Ode to a Nightingale':

> Now more than ever seems it rich to die.
> To cease upon the midnight with no pain.

Well, I didn't die, thanks to the dedication and brilliance of Bart's cardiac team, and in particular Gareth ('The Knife') Rees, who brought in his entire First Eleven on a Sunday to carve up and rebuilt my heart in a triple by-pass operation lasting nine hours.

My staff at the *Express*, said *Private Eye*, were saying the operation took nine hours because it took Gareth eight hours to find my heart! (I think this may be an exaggeration. Gareth, too, believes in sweeping incisions. The scars from his handiwork, on top of those from my splenectomy, make my chest and stomach resemble an aerial shot of Ham marshalling yards before the RAF got at them.)

What conclusions do I draw from all this?

Nothing very profound, I'm afraid.

Clearly, that my time has not yet come. The Bells of Hell went Ting-a-ling-ling, but they did not toll for me.

My life has not altered in any material way. I am not striving to prolong it, particularly. But then I never did. I am, of course, significantly more fatalistic than I once was. *Que sera, sera*, and all that.

I would love to have Faith. I have always envied the serenity of the true believer. Nowadays, burdened as I am from time to time with intimations of mortality, I envy it more than ever.

There is another curious phenomenon. I now have an absolute conviction, for some reason, that my near-death experiences will not be repeated.

Deep in my heart – my battered, bruised but still bravely-beating heart – I know that when I am swept down that long, dark tunnel for a third time I will not be coming back.

I will be travelling home to God – or marching into oblivion. I shall not be afraid.

3

The Rev. Professor Andrew Linzey

Only later did I hear my experiences described as 'mystical' – 'nature mysticism' in particular. At the time I thought them natural. Intense and beautiful – to be sure – but not abnormal. It came as a shock to learn that many did not apparently have these experiences and, even more so, that some people denied that they happened at all.

On reflection I now see that they were unusual. At least in the sense that they were not obviously attributable to my own social conditioning and background. My family were not, to say the least, strongly religious. My religious education was really non-existent. When at the age of fourteen I announced my desire to be ordained, my family reacted – not unnaturally – with incredulity and mirth.

The intensity of the experiences have long since passed, but I now see that they have led to two long-term consequences. The first was the desire to be a priest. That God existed, despite all my personal querulousness and doubt, was never an issue for me as it was for my contemporaries. I believed as someone convinced from early years of the existence of other worlds. There's more in heaven and earth than most people's philosophy was my experience. I have always liked the line from Malcolm Muggeridge that 'a savage prostrating himself before a painted stone has always seemed to me nearer the truth than any Einstein or Bertrand Russell'. I was drawn to theology because its language allowed for the discussion of the apparently incredible.

While the intensity has certainly faded, even now I recollect moments wandering around Oxford (where I lived for the first eighteen years of my life) of sublime illumination. I snatch from my memory glimpses of transfiguration. It would happen as simply as this: sitting, reflecting on the bank of a river or in a wood or in a field, my mind would focus on some natural object and gently a profound sense of well-being would well up within me. An all-pervading sense of the infinite goodness of God the Creator within all living things. An experience of being connected, made whole, one with something Other beyond yet made manifest within every particle of creation. 'Andrew is getting high on nature again' was the understandable – if not entirely accurate – reproach of some of my friends.

The second consequence, though I only see it now in retrospect, was a deepened empathy for the world of nature and a particular sensitivity for animals. I have always been struck by the Christ-like innocence of animals. Although I became subsequently convinced by the rational arguments against animal exploitation, they were never where my sensitivity began. Now, as ever, I am appalled and shocked by the contemporary disregard for animal life. Such feeling is sometimes loosely dismissed as 'neo-pantheism' or, even worse, 'idolatry'. The reverse is the case. It is the Creator who leads us into a deepened awareness of the sacredness of all life. To feel the suffering of other creatures is divine grace.

Reading Albert Schweitzer was a revelation. His theology based on the 'mysticism' of reverence for life made me realise I was not alone. 'There grew in me an unshakeable conviction,' he wrote, reflecting on his own childhood and adolescence, 'that we have no right to inflict suffering and death on another living creature unless there is some unavoidable necessity for it, and that we ought all of us to feel what a horrible thing it is to cause suffering and death out of mere thoughtlessness ... I have grown more and more certain ... that we fail to acknowledge it and to carry our belief into practice chiefly because we are afraid of being laughed at by other people as sentimentalists, though partly also because we allow our best feelings to get blunted.' Schweitzer vowed that he would never disguise his feelings or be afraid of the 'reproach of sentimentalism'.

I too have made a similar vow. And in the process I have found the many-sidedness of theology – despite all its fashionable reductionism – both an illumination and a grace. For at the centre of Christian theology is the Word made flesh, God sentient and crucified. A way of divine power so powerful that it is made real in powerlessness, humility, gentleness and self-costly loving. Sensitivity to God's creation follows inexorably from faith in God the Creator – or should do. I do not know what it means to be a Christian and not to lay before oneself the goal of becoming a more sensitive, gentle, loving, forgiving person.

Our cruel, harsh and exploitative attitude to nature, and animals in particular, stems from spiritual blindness. We do not see that the lives of other living creatures have value and worth beyond our narrow anthropocentric horizons. The truth is that our concept of God is still dreadfully narrow. We have failed to connect, to perceive the significances of other worlds, and to feel their pain. We have lost what D.H. Lawrence once called 'the sixth sense of wonder'.

What I cannot deny is that the Spirit was present in my early experiences in a way that I now see that the Spirit is operative within the whole realm of creation itself. The Spirit which animates all life is also the source of all goodness, beauty and creativity not least in poetry, literature, art, music and thinking. What I once thought was a personal, localised set of experiences in my home town is what I have now come to see as *the* experience open and real to all in every truly creative human experience. 'Whatever we create, however truly it reflects our creation, is always invested with something more powerful than the selves which have produced it,' wrote Laurens van der Post. 'The power and the glory is at our service, but never of our invention.'

4

The Rt. Rev. Robert Hardy

For many of my generation, National Service was a kind of watershed. It stuck across our young adulthood, interrupting careers and education, and for many, like myself, exposing us, for the first time, to a different and a wider world.

Looking back, I had had a pretty conventional upbringing. My home in Wakefield was happy, secure and affectionate, and, my sister being nine years younger, I was brought up virtually as an only child. My father was an accountant in private practice. He worked hard, with long hours at his office. My mother stayed at home. Both my parents were church-goers, popular in the community, and with a wide circle of friends and acquaintances. Yet, looking back, it all appears a much narrower world than the one today. My father walked each day to his office. He came home for lunch. I cycled to school, and on a Saturday or Sunday we would either cycle or drive into the countryside of West Yorkshire, taking a picnic with us. We listened to the wireless a good deal. There were always plenty of books in the house, yet we hardly ever visited the theatre or went to a concert or a gallery. I cannot recall any conversations about religion, sex or politics. My family were not prudish, but they were private. Reticence was highly esteemed.

School itself was somehow an extension of all this. It was hard-working and hard-playing. There weren't many frills. Religion, too, was fairly straightforward. I won a choral scholarship to the Cathedral choir and attended the local grammar school. The Cathedral services were quite formal. They were well-prepared and conducted, but there was no attempt to go beyond this regular round; though I graduated from the choir to become a server, there was little to feed the spirit beyond the pattern of weekly worship. Two individuals stand out from this time in my memory; they opened my life and gave it a glimpse of a wider world. The first was an English master who came, like a breath of fresh air, and introduced us to modern novels and poetry. The second was the Suffragan Bishop of the Diocese, for whom I served regularly early each Wednesday morning in the Cathedral. After the service he would talk to me in a direct and personal way about his own faith, his work and his beliefs. It was the first time any clergyman had done this to me, and it left a significant mark.

I had thought about ordination throughout my latter years at school, but with the prospect of National Service, and the hope of university, did very little about it. So I went off to Cardington, on leaving school, very much with an open mind, recognising that both the RAF and Cambridge might destroy the untried nature of my faith.

The RAF was a revelation. I somehow hadn't realised that there were so many of my contemporaries who were not destined for further education. Many had marvellous practical skills I totally lacked. They created a better sense of community than I had hitherto experienced. So it was a good life – no particular responsibilities, or constraints other than the military ones. For the first time I was largely the master of my own fate and in addition I had money to spend (28s per week!).

After basic training, I was posted to RAF Hereford for training, improbably as a shorthand-typist. The life was comfortable, interesting and varied. There was plenty of sport, good pubs in the locality, enough social life, and an attractive city a bus-ride from the camp. I soon got things organised, and developed an easy pattern of hitch-hiking back to Wakefield every second or third weekend, and then staying on camp for the remainder. It was on one of these camp weekends that I went to Evensong in Hereford Cathedral.

I sat, I remember, at the back of the choir (I could still take you to the spot). I cannot recall any detail of the service, nor can I remember feeling anything in particular about the occasion. I wasn't worried or depressed, nor was I feeling especially pious or seeking anything in particular. But I had an experience of God: that He was real and that He knew me. There was nothing dramatic, no voice or command, and certainly no vision or apparition. There was, however, a definite presence, a disclosure, a positive reassurance, an almost 'tangible experience' – so much so that it has remained vivid and fresh with me until this day. When I came out of that Cathedral, I *knew* that God was very real and that, somehow, a personal relationship existed between us. And that was enough.

Of course I had attended Church many times before my 'experience', and have done so many times since. I suppose, in some ways, my background and my past had prepared me. But the experience has never been repeated, even though I have looked for it, and even, in times of anxiety, actually asked for it in prayer. In one sense, of course, it hasn't been necessary, for, like Elijah, I have gone 'in the strength of that food' for many days. What has been given me instead over the years is an enrichment of the occasion. It has almost become sharper, and certainly more meaningful. It didn't change my life, but it did begin to colour my faith and to undergird my purpose.

In particular the experience has brought me in touch with my feeling for God and my wonder at His graciousness and the appreciation that my own personal relationship with Him is possible. I'm one of those people who believes that religion is all concerned with the faithfulness of God and the unfaithfulness of man. We lose heart in religion because we think we can trust ourselves to be faithful to God. We break down, and then we are discouraged. But religion isn't pretending to be faithful, it is trust – real trust – in the faithfulness of God, and going back to Him again and again for forgiveness and a new beginning. For me, it is all much more a matter of will than of feeling. My Hereford experience made all this possible. It helped me value other men's experience as well, and to see that emotion and will needed to be held together in my belief.

Secondly, the personal nature of the experience underlined for me the matter of judgement: that God knew me, and He cared about how I lived and behaved. Perhaps it is all built on the hard work and diligence of my parents. They wanted me to succeed and, in a way, made me feel accountable. The experience of Hereford transferred that accountability to God, and so it has remained: a permanent part of my own discipleship.

Lastly, the experience gave me a lively sense of the Communion of Saints, that varied company of men and women, living and departed, who have known God and been known of Him. In the words of Richard Baxter's hymn

> He wants not friends that hath thy love,
>   and may converse and walk with thee,
> and with thy saints here and above
>   with whom for ever I must be
>
> Before thy throne we daily meet
>   as joint petitioners to thee;
> in Spirit we each other greet
>   and shall again each other see.

To me, that is always a comfort and a joy. Whatever happens to me, I *know* it is true, and it will not change, thank God.

5

Dame Cicely Saunders

Loss and sorrow can open our eyes and hearts to realities that may be crowded out by a happy or busily occupied life. The challenges of wartime nursing and of the writings of C.S. Lewis and William Temple and Dorothy Sayers' play *The Man Born to be King* led me to a persistent search for an understanding of the Divine. Only a series of losses brought a final irresistible drawing to commitment. Back problems brought an end to a fulfilling career in nursing, extra work to obtain a war degree and finally a painful end to my parents' marriage meant that I was ready to stop striving. I could do no more than let go. A meeting with convinced friends and prayer that experience would be real and lasting brought a totally unexpected reassurance in words heard only in the mind, 'It's not you who has to do anything. I have done it all.' At that moment I felt that God had turned me round – it was for all the world like suddenly finding the wind at one's back instead of battling against it all the time. All the rest, gratitude for forgiveness and purpose, the endless learning and development of what was to be a vocation to found the first modern research and teaching hospice and the meetings with countless hospice patients, stems from that moment.

The Holy Spirit's gift of awareness, the opening of ways to meet the truths of other people and the beauties of creation, does not seem to me to be something that one can grasp, but rather is it to be received unexpectedly, though often given in the course of a persistent and wholehearted search. Pascal said that chance favours the prepared mind and in many years of raising interest and money, I have learnt that this is a constant pattern. It is when working hard in one direction that the totally unlooked-for help arrives from elsewhere.

Still more, I have been made aware when trying to meet with and understand the questions and anxieties of a dying person that a moment of grace may be given to the meeting. Sometimes, one has to wait helplessly beside an anguished or even angry person with no answers to give only to find that quietness has come unexpectedly into the turmoil. The experience of the disciples in the Garden of Gethsemane when they were asked merely to 'watch with me' by their agonised Lord was one of failure to do so, and we will often feel that we, too, have let down those we try to help. Nevertheless I have seen peace come often enough to believe that the God who Himself asked why, and whether the cup could pass from Him, travels this journey with all His children. He met the dangerous and undeserved chances of life with no more than the equipment of a man and gave forgiveness to His torturers to the last. From this comes the endless power of a sacrificial love to share and transform and, I believe, the final answer to the countless victims of random disaster and the indifference and cruelty of others.

Julian of Norwich wrote, 'I saw Him and I sought Him', and although the search and the glimpses of a presence from beyond the everyday world may be hard to separate, yet so often the initiative does not lie with us. Perhaps it never does and the movement of the Spirit is continually within and around us and we have to take only the smallest concern for inner values to open ourselves to seeing those first glimpses that lead on to search.

Jungian analysts have claimed that the figure known as the Genius to the Romans, the Daimon to the Greeks, the Ka to the Ancient Egyptians, the Good Shepherd of the 23rd Psalm, the Comforter (he who makes strong) of St John's Gospel, and the Wayshower of primitive peoples throughout the world is a specific presence directly come upon in modern depth-psychology. When this is followed as a means of exploring the other side of consciousness, they believe there can be a direct encounter with the Friend, the Immortal Companion, the Knower of the Way. I have not sought to learn in that way but I have seen enough among many people nearing death to believe that the experience is not confined but is open to all who seek – agnostics and atheists no less than those who believe. The sole condition seems to be a placing of first things first, the will, however late in life, to reach out trustfully for that which is true.

This was confirmed for me when the Jewish founding patient of St Christopher's died, having left two phrases for reflection on our foundations. One, together with a £500 legacy, was a commission to openness: 'I will be a window in your Home.' The other to a search for skill and wisdom coupled with personal concern: 'I only want what is in your mind and in your heart.' My anxiety at his death that perhaps he had not met with the Truth was fully relieved by another silent word: 'He now knows me far better than you do.' Since then I have felt a deep trust in the often anonymous work of the Spirit for all we have met in the Hospice. The responsibility to care is ours but the final outcome can be safely left in those hands that are 'pierced with unimaginable nails'.

This conviction has grown slowly over the years from reading, prayer and quiet experience. God's sharing with His creation is surely a continuous giving of the freedom of 'one who gives Himself away for the sake of the people He has made'. He suffers with all His children, and in this sharing is given a presence that will finally heal all. 'But all shall be well, and all shall be well, and all manner of things shall be well.'

After my patient and friend died, I suffered deep loss, much healed by another unsought experience some months later. Waking on holiday in a Scottish lodge, I walked along the lochside on a sunny early June morning and sat by a small river running into it. There was a blackbird singing in the woods and peat-stained water running over the glistening granite stones. Without any warning I suddenly slipped out of time. I remember feeling that I had stepped into a timeless Now, that my friend was there somewhere and that it did not matter whether I was near him or not. Somehow we were together in God, he was all right and so was I. This assurance has remained and brought me through other losses since. It is similar to many of the contributions gathered by Sir Alister Hardy's Religious Experience Research Unit in Oxford since 1969.

Years of hospice experience have led us to use the word 'spiritual' rather than 'religious' for what we see and try to facilitate by the giving of space and silent care in which people can feel reaffirmed in their personal value. We aim to see them feel able to say to themselves, 'I'm me and it's all right' before they step from this world into the accepting yet searching Love which many of us believe will meet them.

As a Christian I believe that Jesus comprehends the Way, the Truth and the Life, but I am also convinced that I have seen Him coming to countless people in their own individual way, so often without any words from us. The Divine is totally demanding but yet totally humble in meeting the beginnings of our move towards an eternal reconciliation, fulfilment and thanksgiving.

6

Dame Barbara Cartland

My beloved husband, Hugh, died suddenly on December 29, 1963, one day after we had celebrated twenty-seven years of great happiness.

He was a quiet person who hated publicity, and having loved me for eight years before we were married he was the most contented man I have ever known.

Once I said to him: 'If a fairy could wave a magic wand and give you anything you wanted, what would you wish to have?'

Hugh thought for a moment and replied: 'I have everything I have ever wanted.'

He loved me deeply but he believed that death was the end of everything; there was no after-life, no meeting in another world with those we loved.

After his death I had a message which told me he had been mistaken. I have written down exactly what happened so that it will help other people.

On July 31, 1917 at the Third Battle of Ypres, 2nd Lieut. Hugh McCorquodale received the Military Cross – 'for his gallantry and devotion to duty during the action. It was largely due to his fine personal example and skilful handling of his Company that the enemy counter-attack was delayed.'

My husband was just nineteen years old when he was posted to the 6th Battalion in Flanders. Two months later came the terrible slaughter at Passchendaele.

In this battle the expectation of a subaltern's life was twenty minutes. On July 31 there were 279 casualties in the Battalion, and Hugh was severely – almost mortally – wounded.

In attacking the enemy trenches he was hit with a sniper's dum-dum bullet which passed right through his right shoulder and out of his back exploding as it went. This, among other injuries, collapsed his lung and smashed three ribs. He turned head over heels and lay out in No-Man's-Land for forty-eight hours.

'You were very near to death,' I said to him when we married. 'Did you see angels, hear voices, or even feel you were being helped or sustained?'

'No,' he replied. 'I just felt very tired and far away from all the noise of the battle.'

During the second night Hugh was carried in on a man's back and received a number of shrapnel wounds in the process. At the Field Dressing Station they treated only the shrapnel wounds, not realising he was injured elsewhere.

He was carried down to the Base, but the shelling was so bad that the stretcher-bearers dropped him continually, and when he eventually arrived at No. 9 Red Cross Hospital at Calais he was so covered in mud they did not realise he was an officer and he was at first put in the Tommies' ward.

When the doctors examined Hugh they said there was nothing they could do and there wasn't a chance of his survival. He was therefore, as was the practice in those days, put outside in a tent in the grounds of the hospital by himself to die.

On August 25, his uncle, General Lord Horne (of Stirkoke), who was commanding the First Army, was informed and he sent for Hugh's parents to come over from England to say 'Good-bye' to their son. Mr and Mrs Harold McCorquodale crossed the Channel and saw Hugh for what they thought was the last time.

Hugh had fortunately been taken to a 'rich' hospital which was run by the Canadians, and they gave him port and champagne when they dressed his wounds, and the rest of the time he was under heroin.

He lay for four weeks without food, in a state of semi-consciousness, and we now know that leaving him alone and letting him get over the shock was what saved his life.

After attending five hospitals and having innumerable operations, Hugh survived.

He was a 'show piece' for the doctors, as they considered it a tremendous achievement that they had kept him alive, and he remembered being constantly 'shown off' to visiting specialists.

When he was discharged the doctors said to him: 'It is a miracle you are alive. Nothing more can be done by surgery, so never let anyone fiddle about with you. You must trust to nature and live with your disability.'

It was advice he was to stick to all his life and gave him what amounted to almost a fear of doctors.

Hugh was listed as forty per cent disabled and received a pension which at the time of his death, was £185 16s 0d a year!

His convalescence was very slow and when I met him first in 1927 I was told by various members of his family, including his mother, that he wasn't expected to live long and if he ever got influenza he would die.

We often talked about 'the after-life' especially when Ronald and Tony were both killed at Dunkirk.

'Do you really believe,' I would say to my husband, 'that all Ronald's struggle to help other people is wasted? The times he went hungry so that he could buy books on politics? The years he spent in the Research Department of the Conservative Central Office? The difficulties of money, of working until he made himself ill because he couldn't afford a secretary? Has all that hope, ambition, energy, and faith died with him?'

'I'm afraid so,' my husband would answer.

He was a very quiet, gentle man, who never forced his opinions on anyone, but if I asked him what he thought, he always told me the truth.

On December 29, 1963, after two days of slight bronchitis Hugh got out of bed and collapsed. The scar tissues from the terrible wounds he had received in 1917 had touched his heart.

The day before, though the doctor said there was no need for anxiety, I was instinctively alarmed and I rang Mrs Gibson. I told her about Hugh and she promised to ring me back.

When she did so she said: 'I must be honest, dear, and tell you there is nothing I can do; his time has come. I have covered him in blue and he will pass peacefully.'

I did not believe her and slammed down the telephone.

I had always known Hugh's life hung on a thread and I was deeply grateful for having had him with me for so long.

He did not suffer and for him it was the peaceful, quick death he would have wanted. But that did not assuage the ghastly shock and terrible sense of loss.

I had never seen anyone dead before – all my family had died in France. As I stood beside him as he lay in a blue bed wearing blue pyjamas, I could not believe when he had loved me so much that he had left me alone.

A week after the funeral my maid, who had been with me for over twenty-five years said: 'Have you noticed the wonderful scent of carnations outside Mr McCorquodale's dressing-room?'

'No,' I replied. 'Are you sure? There haven't been any carnations in the house since the funeral and those in the wreaths had no fragrance, not in December.'

'I was so surprised at the strength of the perfume,' my maid went on, 'that I called the daily woman and drew her attention to it. She smelt it too but said it must be something somebody had put in their bath.'

I didn't think any more about this conversation, but the next morning I got up at eight o'clock as usual to give my son Glen his breakfast before leaving for London. There is an entresol with only a skylight outside my bedroom, on to which opened the doors from my husband's dressing-room, his bathroom and the room in which he died.

As I crossed the entresol I was suddenly aware of the marvellous, almost overpowering scent of carnations. It was unlike any carnations I had ever smelt in England – it was the true exotic fragrance of Malmaison which I hadn't known for years.

I stood for a moment feeling astounded, then had to hurry downstairs in case Glen missed his train. When he had gone, I came upstairs and the scent was still there but fainter.

I thought I must have imagined it but the following morning it was there again. It was, I discovered, in patches, the strongest scent being next to my husband's dressing-room. Some mornings it wasn't there at all, or I couldn't smell it until I returned upstairs after breakfast.

The fragrance came and went for three weeks. I asked a friend of mine who had been a medium if she noticed anything, not saying what I was thinking.

She identified the unmistakable scent of Malmaison Carnations and found it all round my bedroom door.

I then knew exactly why it was there. My husband and I had always bought red carnations when we went abroad. Every year we went to Paris for a 'second honeymoon'. The first thing we would do on arrival was to drive to the Madeleine. Outside there are always rows of colourful flower stalls.

Hugh would buy me a huge bunch of red carnations before we went into the Church and said a prayer for our marriage. This was something we had done on our first honeymoon and repeated every year except during the war.

The carnations would be arranged in my bedroom.

Each evening when we went out to dinner Hugh would wear one in his buttonhole.

If anything was a symbol of our happiness and our closeness to each other, it was red carnations. Now I understand why the scent of them was near my door. It could only mean one thing, that Hugh was trying to tell me he had been wrong.

He had found a way to convey to me the truth – there is an after-life, there is survival after death.

7

Tam Dalyell, MP

Quite unashamedly many, not all, great cathedrals cause me to experience the Divine – Durham and Chartres, Lincoln and Autun, Salisbury and Amiens, Canterbury and Bourges, Wells and Rouen, York and Albi, to confine oneself to Britain and France. So do smaller churches, in my West Lothian constituency where people have worshipped for centuries – Abercorn, mentioned by the Venerable Bede, Dalmeny, with its pre-Norman arches, the Quahair at Torphichen, where the Knights Templars built their church, because the area in the twelfth century was a spiritual slum, and the superbly proportioned royal church of the Scots Kings, at St Michael's, Linlithgow, where Mary Queen of Scots was baptised.

I have a similar feeling of the Divine for the Crypt of the House of Commons, albeit that it served as a stable for the horses of Oliver Cromwell's army. The fan-vaulted thirteenth/fourteenth-century edifice goes under three names: St Mary Undercroft, the Chapel of St Stephen, or the Chapel of the Martyrs. Above on the central stones of the vaulting are St Lawrence on his grill, St Margaret and her dragon, St Catherine on her wheel, a Saint in boiling oil whose identity is the source of recondite argument, and St Stephen being stoned. I just have the sense that in this ecumenical church, my predecessors, Members of many Parliaments, Long, Short, or Drunk, by soubriquet, have worshipped, and shared their concerns with God. Certainly, many of them have had their children baptised in the font of Welsh marble, guarded by exquisite marble portraitures of Noah and Moses. The Marian coloured glass of *c.* 1550, whisked out and hidden down a Welsh coal mine for safety in 1941, bears testimony to the vicissitudes of the Crypt. On the wall are the symbols of the Cross, and one of the comparatively few portraits in religious art in Britain of Judas Iscariot, with 29 pieces of silver haloed around him.

I fear, however, I have no such feelings about experiencing the Divine in the Parish Church of the House of Commons, the exquisitely nostalgic St Margaret's, Westminster. I attribute this, partly, to the fact that I must have attended at least a hundred memorial services over thirty years as an MP, for my late colleagues. How those who are chosen to 'do the encomium' from the pulpit is such an abyss of curiosity for most of the audience – yes, audience rather than congregation – that the occasion is robbed of any remote sense of the Divine. The performance is usually tasteful, sometimes mercifully witty, as the deceased would have wished, normally perceptive, seldom hagiographical, but by no stretch of the imagination an experience of the Divine. To experience the Divine, human considerations should be at at least one remove. That is why experiencing the Divine normally occurs for me via contemplation of the wonders of nature.

I first experienced the Divine nature of the rain-forest when I spent my school-teacher's Christmas holidays with the fathers of two of my 14-year-old pupils at Bo'ness Academy on the Forth. David Currie and David Snedden had been coal-miners, who transferred their skills to gold-dredging at Bremang in the Ashanti Forest in Kwame Nkrumah's Ghana. It was the first time I had been in a rain-forest, and by night and by day it captivated me. For the first time I began to appreciate the complex mosaic of what God had created. My friend, who was with me, Richard (now Professor) Layard, became a bit sick. The nearest orthodox doctor was miles away in Kumasi. So, it was resolved that we would try the ju-ju man, or as we called him half in jest, and wholly in earnest, the witch-doctor. His herbal cures and advice worked magic. This incident awoke in me my developing beliefs in the cause of bio-diversity, and the medicinal bountifulness of the Divine. God can operate through the instrument of a ju-ju man, who can neither read nor write. Over thirty years later, with experience of rain-forest in Borneo, Sarawak, Subah, Queensland, Burma, Zaire, Belize, and the Amazon, I was to appreciate the skills of Dr Elaine Elizabetsky and her Brazilian colleagues at the Goeldi Institute at Belem, who are contributing new dimensions to medicine.

Probably it is fierce competition in the struggle to survive that has caused nature to create a whole range of chemical compounds used by rain-forest animals, insects, and plants for attack, defence, sexual attraction and repulsion, and a host of other purposes. The forest-dwelling tribal people's knowledge of medicines derived from the wild is, like that of my ju-ju friend of over thirty years ago, astonishing. To the Ibans of Sarawak, as to the Kayapo Indians of Brazil, and thousands of other peoples, the forest is an embracing natural pharmacy. They use a real medicine chest of plants and animal/insect products for serious illness and contraception; they can deal with foot-rot, impotence and the whole range of other sicknesses of the rain-forest.

The chemical library which is the rain-forest has been, but should be used more by Western medicine, and our great pharmaceutical companies. As it is, about one in four of all purchases from chemists in Britain contain an active ingredient derived from a tropical forest species. Our advanced medical treatments also depend on rain-forest products. These include drugs to treat bronchitis, cancer, dysentery, heart diseases, hypertension, malaria and tuberculosis. The products include anaesthetics, antibiotics, antiseptics, contraceptives, enzymes, hallucinogens, hormones and laxatives. The rain-forest helps Western medicine in four general ways. First, chemicals extracted from plant and animal species can be used without modification as drugs. Synthesis may be impossible if scientists cannot unravel the biochemical process, or perhaps it may not be commercially feasible if natural sources are cheaper. Secondly, some extracts of rain-forest plants and animals may serve as the starting point for the manufacture of semi-synthetic derivative drugs. Thirdly, other extracts provide chemical models or blueprints which pharmacists use to develop synthetic compounds. Divine nature gives insights, through her complex natural molecules, which may be beyond the capabilities of even the most brilliant human researchers. Lastly, plant and animal species, or extracts from them, may be used for research purposes.

At the 1989 Altamira rally of the American-Indian tribes – the first occasion many of them had ever come together – in the Xingu, I met people whose malaria had been treated with the bark on cinchona trees. Two hundred years went by between the discovery of this treatment by Europeans and the identification of the alkaloid quinine. Now, with the rise in malaria, the bark is proving a better medicine than synthetic drugs. This is the kind of example which leads me to believe in the concept of divine help.

Many tropical forest plant and animal derivatives are used in the vital functions of relieving pain and assisting in the performance of surgical operations. From Erythroxylon Coca, a South American coca bush, comes cocaine, important as a local anaesthetic, and a blueprint for safer anaesthetics such as novocaine and lignocaine. When I was in the Yucatan Peninsula in Mexico, I saw Mexican yams, which do not flourish outside rain-forests, which are a source for diosgenin. In turn diosgenin is the basic material for the manufacture of many steroidal drugs including the birth-control pill and the sex hormones progesterone, oestrogen and androgens. The yam also provides the semi-synthetic derivatives cortisone and hydrocortisone, which treat arthritis, eye inflammation, skin diseases and rheumatic fever. Another South American legume, the Mucuna, produces L-dopa, a neurotransmitter naturally occurring in the human brain, which is used to combat the disabling effects of Parkinson's disease.

My sense of the Divine tells me that rain-forests, and indeed temperate forests, are essential to the survival of life. The extensive historical deforestation by developed countries contributed to our economic growth. I fear deforestation continues because the factors that cause deforestation are not easily eliminated; these causes are primarily related to the unsustainable consumption patterns in developed countries, inadequate prices for forest produce below the full replacement cost, debt burden, and the general poverty of developing countries.

I believe that developed countries have a sacred responsibility for restoring and maintaining an adequate level of global forest cover. This responsibility applies both within the territory of developed countries, and to compensation of efforts by rain-forest countries without conditionality.

Experiencing the Divine imposes its own obligations on those who are the fortunate recipients of such an experience. That is why I feel bound to participate in the congregation of those in many countries who are endeavouring to save the rain-forest.

Experiencing the Divine involves guardianship. When I heard Martin von Hildebrand, rain-forest adviser to the President of Colombia, address a meeting at the Museum of Ethnology in London, the concept of guardianship came home to me. No one in the Colombian reserve could kill an animal without consulting the Guardian of the tapirs or whatever animal was under discussion. So, in our society, I believe that we should at least consult ourselves about guardianship of our planet, before taking any action that would harm the planet irretrievably. If we are to experience divine nature, then we have to practise our obligations to the Divine.

8

The Rt. Rev. Lord Coggan

That giant of a man, Paul the Apostle, wrote of 'visions and revelations granted by the Lord', of being 'caught up as far as the third heaven', of being 'elated by the magnificence of such revelations' (II Corinthians 12:1, 2, 7). The writer of this essay can describe no such things, and the reader of it must look elsewhere in this book if he wants such disclosures of the Divine. I make no claim to have scaled the heights. I am an earthy type. That may well be my fault – too much an activist, too little a visionary. It may, in part, be due to the genes I have inherited. Conceivably, it might be in the purpose of God – the way he deals with a rather humdrum servant. I do not know. Perhaps it does not matter overmuch. It might even turn out to be an advantage, for what I shall write of my own experience may help others whose contacts with the Divine partake more of the slog than of the eagle's flight.

That is not to say that there have been no moments when the veil between this world and that has become thin. Iona has been described as a 'very thin' place, and I think I know what that means – *there* are history and sanctity and beauty in a rare combination. C.B. Rootham or George Guest in St John's Chapel, Cambridge, in charge of Bach's 'Jesu, Joy of man's desiring'; a mighty rendering in Canterbury Cathedral of Parry's 'I was glad'; some orchestral gift of Beethoven or Mozart which leaves you with a conviction that, somehow, things at the heart of the universe are all right; or again – with Browning – 'there's a sunset touch' – are not these disclosures of the Divine into which we are invited to enter? Wonder, it has been said, is next to worship – the two intermingle. It does not take a great cathedral to lead to such an experience; a country congregation with a man or woman of God in charge, a faithful ministry of word and sacrament that may lack the finesse which a trained choir or a brilliant organist can offer, *there* can be a disclosure of the Divine, and I have experienced it.

At the heart of the Eucharist, at its simplest or at its most elaborate, is the central communication of the love of God going out to us and seeking our response – the divine contract is renewed, an answer is sought:

Thou gavest thyself for me.
I give myself to thee.

Here is life's meeting-point with the Divine, the corporate and the individual in a wonderful combination, the Church at its central task of worship, the individual in a response which he or she alone can make. More often than not, that renewal of contract between God and man is accompanied by little human emotion, but who is to say that that lack of emotion inhibits the reality of the contract or the experience of the divine? The angels of God ascend and descend the ladder (John 1:51) even when our eyes are too dim to see them or our ears too deaf to hear the flutter of their wings.

'Each piece should be written from the author's own perspective, ideally drawing upon personal experiences.' These were the editor's instructions to the writers of these essays. So be it, I will obey. Looking back over my life, I think it would be true to say that very many of my experiences of the Divine – at least regarded from the pragmatic viewpoint of the difference they have made in daily life – have been the result of study of and meditation upon the Bible. That is not to say that, in the time set aside for such reading, flashes of brilliant truth or experiences of the Divine are given every day. Far from it. Sometimes there is such a flash – 'I had never seen it quite like that before.' But far more frequently the meditation seems to have no immediate result. Does that mean that nothing is happening? I don't think so. One's physical strength is derived from the steady consumption of ordinary food, not from those meals which can only be described as exquisite. From the daily pondering on Scripture in its breadth and depth emerge principles of life and truth by which character is made and decisions are less frequently disastrous. When you come to the crossroads, it is easier to hear the voice that says 'This is the way, walk ye in it', and to avoid the path that leads to destruction.

When these principles of life and truth become part and parcel of one's attitude to life, it is a fact of experience that, when the hurricanes blow, one finds one's way to the peace which is at the centre of the storm. A certain serenity is given to displace fear. Perhaps the nearest I came to 'hearing a voice from heaven' was at a critical time during the war. Taking up a new post in London, the future largely unknown, wife and family left abroad, I was travelling through the night by train. 'You have not chosen me, I have chosen you and ordained you' – the words repeated themselves as the train rolled on through the blackout. So far as I recall, I had not been specially thinking of them before. But that night they came as a benediction, an assurance, an undergirding. Explain this as you will, could we not call it an experience of the Divine?

'Guidance' is part and parcel of the vocabulary of the Christian. I do not find it an easy concept. But I am compelled to accept it as a reality, for again and again it seems to be an authentic part of the experience of men and women who seek to walk with God. More often than not, it is a reality which can only be recognised *after* the particular event – one looks back and sees how disastrous or how limiting it would have been if the other course had been followed. But there was a real seeking for the mind of God and a readiness to obey. *Looking back*, one can discern a pattern, a design, which at the time was known only to God. Perhaps the crux is in the word 'obey'. 'Whoever has the will to do the will of God shall know ...' (John 7:17) – there is profound truth there. 'Has the will', even in the little things. 'The only recipe for emergent heroism is faithfulness in little things' – so wrote a gallant pioneer woman missionary. It is a fact of religious experience that, when a person gets into the habit of being obedient in small matters to the dictates of an enlightened conscience, when the crisis or the big decision comes he will walk with firm step.

There is another channel through which the experience of the Divine is mediated to us, and I certainly have entered into this. One has the opportunity of meeting people far further on the road of discipleship, living obviously in much closer friendship with God than one is oneself. Such people themselves are windows into the nature of God. Their lives rebuke us, humble us, stimulate us, egg us on. Call this what you will – a sharing in the fellowship of the Spirit, participating in the Body of Christ – it is a reality. Nor is it confined to those still physically with us. The recollection of those we have known, and the 'friendship' with men and women of God long since departed but made known to us through the medium of biography – these also provide us with experiences of the Divine. They are windows into God. They mitigate the loneliness of discipleship.

Two further things must be said: First, for the writer of this essay, the person of Jesus Christ has been, and is, central to his experience of the Divine. In him, he sees God focused in a way which he finds nowhere else – God's immensity made available, God's heart and mind disclosed, God's love and grace offered and provided in the incarnate, crucified and risen Lord. Paul was surely commenting on his own experience of the divine when he wrote: 'The God who said "Out of darkness light shall shine" has caused his light to shine in our hearts, the light which is knowledge of the glory of God *in the face of*

Jesus Christ' (II Corinthians 4:6). Secondly, the writer is provided with a *hope*. Now, the experience of the Divine is incomplete, I had almost said fleeting, transitory. But one day we shall see 'face to face'. The Revised English Bible puts the passage in I Corinthians 13 well: 'At present we see only puzzling reflections in a mirror, but one day we shall see face to face. My knowledge now is partial; then it will be whole, like God's knowledge of me' (v. 12). Perhaps that says it all. Not all that I would *like* to know, but all that I *need* to know. It is enough to keep me on the road, enough to keep me wondering and worshipping and stretching forward to the day when fleeting experiences of the Divine give way to the glorious vision of God. This, all down the centuries, has been at the centre of the Christian's hope and its abiding inspiration.

9

Sister Francis Dominica

I found him in the hills, rugged, eternal, untouched by the strivings and turmoil of humankind five miles and a million years away. I found him on the shore, the wind in my ears deafening me to all other sound, wisps of white cloud scudding across a deep blue sky, matched in their brilliance only by the sea horses coming towards me from as far away as my eye could see.

Then I recognised him sitting beside me. He had the face of a woman, her eyes red and swollen with crying, body trembling with grief. Three days ago her children had been buried. After years of sickness and suffering caused by a rare genetic illness the two little boys had died only a few days apart. Her marriage broken a few months before, she no longer had husband or children. 'I am nobody's wife,' she said. 'There's no one to call me Mum any more. It's strange, I'm not sure who I am.'

I had known them several years. I think the liking and respect I had for her was reciprocated but she had not shared much by way of feelings, choosing to stay a little apart from us, head held high, determined at all costs to remain in control of her children's lives, unafraid to challenge the most venerable paediatrician if the treatment he prescribed puzzled her or was in conflict with her intuitive judgement. It was only afterwards she told me that her single-minded drive to be in control was her desperate bid to keep hold of sanity. It was only afterwards she told me her closely-guarded secret, of the abuse she had suffered at the hands of her husband throughout their marriage, and showed me the scars she still carries.

She had little time for deceit or hypocrisy. The only place for pretence was in the safe and beautiful world of her children's fantasy and imagination which she entered with ease and with childlike joy. At other times unadulterated truth was what she gave and believed it was her right to receive. She talked straight and she lived straight and expected others to do the same.

There was no nobility about her, even now in her brokenness. Her compassion had been woven into every detail of practical day-to-day living for the children, the edges never blurred by sentimentality. I had known her compassion myself the night the body of the first child was carried from the house, the younger child waving from the window just as he had done so many times before when the transport had come to take his brother to school. I stood on the pavement sobbing and it was she who put her arms around me and comforted and strengthened me.

Her love for her boys overrode any consideration for herself and her needs. 'How do you cope?' people would ask, amazed at her ability to keep going through the relentless round of caring for the boys day after day and broken night after broken night. 'No one gave me a choice,' she would reply, often with a smile, while she continued with the task in hand. Only the best was good enough for her boys. Money was short, but the best did not usually mean the best that money could buy anyway. She knew very well that expensive toys and gifts held her children's attention for a brief moment only and did little to strengthen their security or reinforce their awareness of her love for them. Only the gift of herself could do that and of herself she gave without hesitation and without counting the cost, hour by hour, day by day, year after year. This was sacrificial love.

And now there was nothing. Family and friends who had gathered for the last hours of those young lives and for the funeral had scattered now and gone their various ways. There had been so much to do while the children still lived and when they died, always so much to do. And now there was nothing. Sitting beside her in the quiet, empty house, I felt an acute physical pain in the very centre of my being. Perhaps it was symbolic of the small fraction of pain I had absorbed of her immense, immeasurable pain. She sat there dressed in jeans and trainers, an ordinary woman with her share of faults and weaknesses. But I had seen other things – nobility, truth, compassion, sacrificial love. These are intrinsic to the God I worship. In that face ravaged with grief I looked into the eyes of my God.

*

It did not end there. Every now and then I am caught unawares. Sometimes it is a child, sometimes a woman, sometimes a man, of black skin or white, young or old. It may be someone with whom I share similarities of background or experience, of faith or politics, or it may not. But usually in the midst of ordinary, run-of-the-mill life, often in the presence of suffering, I catch a glimpse and I know that my encounter, however brief, has been with the Divine.

10

The Rt. Hon. Sir Rhodes Boyson, MP

I grew up in a large Non-conformist family in a small village and small town in east Lancashire which took for granted the existence of God and his presence in our daily lives. From my earliest days I heard the Bible read at home and in church and many of my relatives carried Biblical names like Jabez and Ezekiel.

The first ten years of my life were spent in a village of some 1,500 people and my life centred round the village Methodist Church, the village Anglican School and my large family of Methodist and Baptist believers. The only real split was between Non-conformists and Anglicans, although we tolerated and even were close friends with many Anglicans! It was a blessed and secure experience to grow up in a warm society where there were no arguments with atheists and agnostics, although mention was made at times of people in the village having strange views and of some who did not even attend church!

My mother believed that by prayer all things could be achieved. At one stage there developed a large lump in her breast, she prayed that this would be removed and encouraged the rest of her family to similar prayers. The lump disappeared, to the amazement and annoyance of our local doctor, and mother had no doubt its disappearance was the work of the Almighty. I went to church and Sunday School three times every Sunday and read the Bible daily, and God was close to me as he was in the Heavens. Mother was Superintendent of the Sunday School and taught a young ladies' class on one evening a week. My father organised and chaired a Sunday afternoon class which was packed on most occasions. Forgive the break in sequence, but my mother lived to ninety-one and she continued living for the last few months until she could lay a foundation stone again of the replacement village chapel where she had spent so much of her life. Then she died grateful to the Almighty.

When I was ten we moved to the main 14,000 population town and we took membership of another Methodist Church, now sadly closed. Father was the town's Labour leader and we were welcomed into the new church where again we attended regularly.

Political thought and activity began to fill part of my life in early adolescence. Father was a full-time trade union secretary. The clouds of war were spreading over Europe and we received the monthly edition of the Left Book Club like the epistles of St Paul, although father took and insisted I read the Right Book Club publications as well so that I understood both sides of the question.

My religion and my politics then became mixed and at seventeen I received a note to preach and began to take services. I even thought of becoming a Methodist minister. I joined the Royal Navy, however, instead.

Before then I had, however, one experience where I felt the very presence and help of the Almighty. I had become perplexed about one issue of faith and behaviour which worried me. One Sunday evening – I was about fifteen years old – I announced I would not go to church that evening and said I would pray at home. I did, and after half an hour my mind was cleared as in a blinding flash and I knew exactly what to do and the worry and concern were totally lifted from me and never returned. I shall never forget that evening.

In the sixth form at school we had a debating society, and religious and political issues were discussed at length. I never felt any doubt of the existence of God, nor did the vast majority of my friends. We could discuss religion dispassionately, but we overwhelmingly had faith and we almost all attended church or chapel.

It was about this time that I realised the difference between my mother's and my father's faith. My mother – like Lord Shaftesbury – felt the presence of God in every room at every moment, but father intellectually felt that there must be a God. Mother's faith was of the heart, my father's of the mind.

I always felt close to God while I walked by myself the hills of the Rossendale Valley, where my mother's ancestors had lived and farmed and worshipped for generations.

I regularly worshipped in the Royal Navy, and when I returned to civilian life it was back to my home town, to the same church, to the same Labour Party and to the same hill.

My personal divergence from the Labour Party came partially on religious grounds. I had in the Royal Navy and afterwards become much more aware of the fall of man. The Garden of Eden was still alive in the lives of people and of nations and I became much more aware that men and women were fallen creatures only to be saved by grace.

I read the Bible regularly, pray both regularly and irregularly and at times of crisis lean on my religious beliefs. I remember the Cuban-USA-Russian missile crisis and I think I would have been in deep despair apart from my religious faith.

I also attend church services regularly with my wife in my constituency and also attend and occasionally worship on Saturday at the synagogues in Brent North. I follow carefully the readings in the Jewish scriptures and check the footnotes for further information and often gain acute religious insights. One week, which was exceptional, I attended a Muslim service on a Friday, a Jewish service on the Saturday and a Christian service on the Sunday in my constituency.

I still take at least one Methodist service a quarter and last year I was greatly honoured to take part in the covenant service at Wesley's Chapel. As I climbed the steps of the pulpit the whole of my life came back to me: the village chapel, my mother, the hills of Rossendale. Similarly I am honoured to be Chairman of the Methodists in the Commons.

'Experiencing the Divine' means to me that we live life on two planes. One is the necessary daily round and common task. The second is the fact that this life is but a part of a whole and that by thoughtful prayer and faith we can, as it were, live on two levels – the workaday one below, which can be guided and helped by setting it against the background of the Divine.

One final point. I was privileged to grow up in a believing, Christian home and to be immersed in religion from my earliest days. I am sorry that, with the decline of religious education in schools and in church attendance, fewer people now have this privilege which must lead many to 'experiencing the Divine'.

11

Peter Mullen

My 'experience of the Divine' is taken from my autobiographical novel. This should not make any difference because even a fictionalised account must in the end be based on experience. But lest I offend anyone's ontological scruples by quoting from a mere novel, I should say that my 'experience' did in fact happen just as I have written it.

*

In the teenage Confirmation Class, Father Thornton said, 'God is in love with mankind.'

'Well, well, well.'

Anne shuffled on her seat. The others – Phil Foster and Roger Hodgson – looked interested. But to Peter it was a radical shift, like a bomb under the Chapel. The shock was physical as well as emotional: it was as if someone had rolled away the sepulchral stone. So, actual tangible things, people even, are sustained by love, are they?

'God cannot stop loving the world. It's against His nature. He loves us forever.'

'What – even if you've done something really rotten?' Peter blurted out.

'Like what?'

He could feel his cheeks turning a hot colour. He trod water: 'Oh anything, you know. Anything really bad.'

'Huh? Huh?' And a great incense cloud of Bruno 'Like crucifying Him. Huh? And what did he say then? Tell me that. Huh? Huh?'

Demurely Anne said, 'Father forgive them. They know not what they do.'

Outside in the dark, St Bartholomew's Church loomed over the suburb like a Victorian grandparent. He walked Anne home and told her he liked the kilt.

'Did you enjoy it?'

His mind was on the kilt and the ivory blouse. 'The class – did you enjoy it?'

'Yes.' He did not feel there was much he could say.

When he had seen her home, he had to walk back past the Church.

It was black, huge, a mock Gothic cathedral on a hill. You could see it from all over Leeds. He wondered why he had never been in it. The moonlight shone through the lattice work in the tower. The graveyard had been full for a long time.

He said a few prayers in bed that night, tentatively, self-consciously. It was difficult to account for the happy state of mind. Fancy praying not to someone whose wrath could barely be turned aside, but to someone who, as it said on the inside front cover of the Confirmation Manual given out by Father Thornton, 'art always more ready to hear than we to pray, and art wont to give us more than we either desire or deserve ...'

He laughed out loud like the woman who found her lost coin. Complementaries. Parallelisms. Alliteration. He had heard it all from Geoff Rans. But that was what you did with alliteration, was it, 'desire or deserve'?

Sunday morning and he entered St Barts during the singing of the Introit. Here comes the gold cross, the Crucifer in his alb and behind him the choir in red and white. Servers, acolytes, the Vicar and the two Curates in green vestments. The very marks of the beast. Except there was no beast, only beauty. They were singing 'Blessed City Heavenly Salem' to the tune 'Westminster' (A and M Revised 620). It was as if he had died and gone to heaven and, moreover, had found it void of Evangelical Retribution. The Schultze organ, crowned with the carved angel of the Apocalypse, growled and roared. Then it calmed down, sounded like a single clarinet in Paradise over the words:

From celestial realms descending,
Bridal glory round thee shed,
Meet for him whose love espoused thee,
To thy Lord thou shalt be led ...

It could not be true, could it? Then there was a roar of bass notes and a terrifying improvisation by the organist in the last verse:

Laud and Honour to the Father
Laud and Honour to the Son ...

Fathers and Sons coupled together. It could not be true, could it? Blood was thicker than water, though. The prayers began: 'O God, forasmuch as without thee, we are not able to please thee ...'

Complementaries. Parallelisms. After a short sermon from the Vicar, which was amusing so that some people even laughed here and there, it was the Communion. Not a hole-and-corner affair, after Divine Service on the Fourth Sunday in the month – Ribena in individual glasses, brought round by frosty Deacons to where you were sitting – but a going forward to the high altar. An aromatic blend of ritual and red wine. Eight candles flickering. The Schultze again, restrained: 'Let All Mortal Flesh Keep Silence'. Another prayer and then Haydn: 'Praise the Lord, Ye heavens Adore Him', and in the silence a holy thump as the congregation knelt. The silence shattered by the summons to action that begins Bach's 'Toccata and Fugue in D Minor'.

Religion without condemnation. Religion with real music. Religion that was not a denial of colour and light. It did not seem possible. Well, even if it turned out to be impossible, Peter knew he would stick with it: there was nowhere else to go, 'Is it always like that?' he asked Rod Boom as they were on the way to The White Horse that night.

'Like what?'

'Terrific, you know. Incredible.'

'It's a nice church.'

A nice church! It was like saying the K. 309 was 'only scales'.

In Webbs warehouse on Monday morning he met Elsie Dawson coming in, shaking her yellow brolly. 'D'you go to church, Mrs Dawson?'

She gave him an odd look. 'I used to.'

He wanted to say that he was sure it would do her good, but teenage boys do not speak like that to mature, unhappy ladies of forty-five.

12

The Rev. Professor David Martin

When I was about nine, in 1938, I was listening to *Children's Hour*. It was a dramatised version of the life of Handel. As the story concluded they started to play the 'Hallelujah Chorus'. I had never heard this kind of music before and started to go into shock. As the trumpet initiated the sequences leading to the climactic high G I was overwhelmed with a delicious and increasing discomfort so difficult to contain that I started to blush with embarrassment and wanted to rush from the room in a flood of unboyish tears. I also recollect that my mother and a visitor went on talking while this occurred, which added to my confusion because I imagined they must be hearing what I heard and would stop everything out of sheer amazement.

Looking back on this experience, I think the shock was so great because church choirs, organs and Sunday school music had provided me with the required musical language yet without any experience of a major composer or for that matter of serious performance. The result was that I suddenly drank the western musical experience 'neat'. I heard the 'Choirs of New Jerusalem' direct and unframed, with immediate recognition but without the shrouding of familiarity.

*

In June or July 1948 I was an acutely unhappy conscript living in a brutally run camp on a hill above the Severn between Stourport and Bewdley. By taking short walks you could find sweet relief by the river or look longingly towards the Wyre Forest and Clee Hill. One weekend I decided to escape and visit friends of my mother's who lived about thirty miles away, near Ludlow. The bus to Ludlow ran from nearby Kidderminster, and as soon as I got on I fell asleep and started to dream, my head constantly hitting a small knob on the bus window. I was not in a good state. But as I stepped off the bus in Ludlow I had clearly entered a New World, where every shape and every particular thing and all human beings, myself included, were imbued with inclusive joy. The world was marvellously ordered according to 'kinds'. The distinctions were not those of old or young, attractive or unattractive, but simply different ways and modes of kindly being. As

I walked around the streets I was drawn by wonder, not interest, observation or curiosity. An exchange of words with one of the other human creatures required no content, since it was just a shared acknowledgement of existence and a kind of angelic salutation.

It seemed 'meet and right' to walk for a moment into the church, and I then wandered into the greensward of the castle, recollecting only a plaque saying 'Milton's *Comus* was first performed here in 1634'.

To get to where my mother's friends lived in the village of Ashford Carbonel was quite a walk from Ludlow, but I barely noticed it. Every now and then I felt inclined to touch things just to register the grain and texture of their existence. On arrival the husband greeted me, and I was fascinated, even a little shocked, at his brilliant white hair and patient face. I remember little about the visit, except a sense of quiet after-joy, especially in the plain and clean little upstairs bedroom. By the bed was a book, of a kind I would (then) have normally ignored. It was *A School of Prayer* by Olive Wyon, bound in SCM green. But picking it up I found a kind of correspondence with the paradisal consciousness I had just passed through, and read it almost as a continuation of the experience.

*

In June 1956 I had just come out of a series of acute and deeply troubling domestic difficulties with my (late) first wife. For some relief I walked with an old school friend Leslie Smith along the South Coast, first from Downderry to Megavissey and then from Osmington Mills to Poole. Arriving in Poole in the middle of Sunday I saw a notice outside Poole Methodist Church: 'Hell is other people' (J.P. Sartre). Leslie was not a church-goer and I was distinctly intermittent in attendance, but the theme certainly touched a nerve. So I went, and immediately on sitting down found myself quietened. I read one or two hymns, and listened attentively to a fine address about hell and other people. Then the choir started to sing a setting of Herbert's 'King of Glory, King of Peace' and in the course of it I felt myself gently invaded by assurance, restitution, recovery, acceptability and reposeful joy. It was all 'taken account of', disposed, underwritten, covered by graciousness. Nothing was required of me. An inner transformation took place, and as I left the church this must have shown on my face because Les remarked on it, saying, 'I've been down to the docks but I haven't had whatever it is you have just had.'

*

In late March 1977 I was coming home to England from Washington, feeling very exhausted. As I settled in on a (British) plane the chief steward announced in a rich plummy voice: 'Her Majesty's Government expects ...' I forget what HMG expected of me, but I heard the words with an almost tearful pleasure. Perhaps 'majesty' and 'government' and 'expects' set off subterranean linkages. I don't know. Then I had a whisky and the pilot said, 'The lights of Philadelphia are there, over to your left.' So there was the City of Brotherly Love, clear and lighted up, as you would expect. The plane purred on into the Atlantic dark and I flicked on the music. Charles Groves was talking about Janet Baker singing a Mahler song at Barbirolli's *Requiem Mass* in Westminster Cathedral. The song was 'Ich bin der Welt abhanden gekommen'. It began with low heart beats on the strings until the voice made its own entry, low and slow at first but beginning to soar upwards with more and more passionate consolations and benedictions, till it sank back to a unity and to mere pulsations. Then the inner world moved to King's, Cambridge, and a singing of the Fauré *Requiem*. 'In Paradisum deducant angeli ... et cum Lazaro ...' – carrying and holding music – and then on again to the exuberant affirmativeness of Mozart's E flat Horn Concerto.

The red of dawn just touched the outer wing and the plane nosed calmly on. The light grew and I realised that everywhere (without location) and at all times, without contrast of holy and profane, the heavens overflowed with this plenitude of being. After perhaps five hours of ecstatic passage I told myself to remember that these 'courts' did not cease to be 'there' when I was no longer standing in them. The ordinary dubiety of God would surely reassert itself in the everyday world. Indeed it did. Heathrow made me extremely mundane and irritable. But all the same I remembered not to forget.

13

Rabbi Julia Neuberger

Like many young people, girls in particular, I had a deeply religious stage in my early teenage years. I became, in rapid succession and to my parents' great irritation, an orthodox Jewess, a committed atheist, a deist and lastly a reform Jewess who 'knew' God. I didn't know God of course. Like many others, I experienced the presence of the Divine in nature, in the magnificent landscape of the blue gault clay of the 1928 landslip near our cottage on the Isle of Wight. I experienced the Divine in love, romance, sex – something so wonderful had to be divinely created. And I lost the divine presence when first faced with real deprivation in Nottingham on the St Anne's project in the mid-sixties, and at other times when I wondered, as we all did, how a just God could allow such things to happen.

That sense has never really left me. Starvation in Africa. Deprivation in the homelands of South Africa so intense that our rubbish was welcomed as a generous gift, the revelations about cruelty in Cambodia, in Vietnam, among the Ibo, in East Timor, let alone our own destruction in the death camps of the Nazis ... all these horrors perpetrated by human beings upon one another, or apparent natural disasters which always affected the poorest most acutely, seemed evidence that if there was a God, he was not a good God, not a kindly God, not a just God.

But in later life, from my days as a student at Cambridge onwards, I have begun to have a different sense. It began with my first visit to a hospice with a Cambridge friend and his father, Dr Donald Richards, an Oxford general practitioner, who had been highly instrumental in setting up the Sobell Hospice on the Churchill Hospital site in Oxford. We went and walked round the hospice and saw its facilities, met its staff, and began chatting to some of the patients. These were the early days of hospices, in the early seventies. Techniques of pain control, in comparison with what we have now, were also in their infancy. But here were patients, largely with cancer, whose last days and months were being made tolerable, if not pleasurable, by pain control so carefully estimated that they were able to get on with the rest of their lives.

The wonderment at the skills of those who work in hospices, from doctors and nurses to cleaners and volunteer receptionists, has never ceased to happen for me. But the sense of the Divine was not in what they had achieved in terms of pain relief, in terms of care and love and support for these terminally ill people, but what they had freed them to do. For they had allowed these people to set their lives in order, to sort out their past lives and do what they still had to do, even wanted to do, in the short future remaining to them.

It was in what some of those people chose to do with their remaining days, weeks or months that I began to experience the Divine. It was not all at once, nor was it the case for every person I spoke to, or for every patient I met. All too few gave me that intense sense of the divine presence. But many of them allowed me a glimpse of it, in how they were coping with their destiny, in how they were talking with their parents, siblings, spouses, children, about their mortality and impending death. Often it was just a shadow I saw, a shadow in the mention of the expectation of peace, of the sense of order, of current business being completed. There were lovers reunited, or families, estranged over some ridiculous imagined slight, brought together at the bedside. There were moments of sublime beauty, when a particularly admired singer came to sing to a woman who was dying and could no longer speak, a moment which brought a lump to my throat and to the throats of all of us there – but also gave us a sense that God is good, and was there on that afternoon, present in the voice of the singer as she sang from *Tosca*, in a hospice of all unlikely places, with greater passion than ever heard on the stage of Covent Garden.

There were amusing moments, with a sense of the presence of a God who could see the joke, when a young man dying of testicular cancer longed for a last football match and a game was played along the corridor of a ward, in wheelchairs, with all the staff helping to get the chairs suitably placed for the ball – and a window got broken, reminding us all of what we had been told as children about not playing with balls inside the house!

Over the years, there have been so many moments where I have felt a shadow of the Divine, in the incredible goodness of the carers, in the acceptance and organisation of those who are about to die, in the humour and pathos of the general situation. But there is something more. In the very encounter with the dying and their families, and later with the bereaved, I have felt a sense of the divine presence. It's not exactly in me. In my somewhat simplistic theology, or perhaps more accurately my somewhat peasant-like belief system, I have always regarded my conscience as God's voice within me in some way. Instead, this sense of the divine presence is round about me, cradling me, comforting me in the bleak moments, making it tolerable to watch the intolerable, the slow gasping dying of a child, making it possible to be with that child's parents, and somehow, God knows how, provide some comfort by my presence.

But the divine presence is not only there at the particularly hard moments. It is there when I sit with the dying, as they die peacefully, painlessly, slipping away into the unknown. It is there at an earlier stage, when we are talking and laughing over some matter they longed to discuss. It is there when I talk with the bereaved who are calming after the death, and whose lives can begin to return to a normal pattern, despite their loss. It is there when I watch the cleaners arrange the flowers on the window-sill, or chat to the patients when they are cleaning the floors.

It is there when I am with the dying and their nearest and dearest. I do not know why. I only know that I find a sense of the nearness of God and a sense of ineffable peace when I am with the dying and the seriously ill, and that my faith is strengthened by that very work. Yet by all rhyme and reason my faith should be challenged by the apparently meaningless death of a child, or by the young man who dies three years into his marriage, leaving a small baby and a 2-year-old child as well as a young, poorly provided for, widow, or by the young mother dying in her late thirties leaving three children whose lives are scarred by the memory of her last and lengthy illness. Why does God allow such things?

I do not know. Sometimes I simply think that is the wrong question. God does not allow or disallow. It is up to us to try to prevent or cure illness, as well as realising that we have to die of something – we are not immortal. But even if it were the right question, and I still ask it myself and hear it so often from those who are dying, and their loved ones who watch them do so. Why me? Why you? Why any of us? In that emotional questioning, in that pain and sorrow, I find God. I find God in the ability sometimes to bring comfort. I find God in the fact that they are able to accept, and come to terms. I find God in the way they are cared for and loved, in the great human goodness tragic situations can evoke. I find God in the lives and work of those who work with the dying. And I find God, very personally, in my encounters with the dying, in my conversations with them, in finding out about their faith. In their faith, my faith is strengthened. It is immaterial which religion they are from, or none. It is in the nature of their faith, so often expressed, that 'it will be all right'. I do not know whether it will be all right myself. But I find God there in their assertion, and in the legacy they leave behind with their families and friends, and in the work that their carers do with them. In death I find life. That's more of a Christian paradox than a Jewish one. But for me, I find the life of the spirit strengthened by the experience of the dying, and by the sense of peace, and love, that is often to be found in the rooms and homes and hospices where they breathe their last.

Part II

Personal Experiences

14

The Rev. Canon Anthony Phillips

I have always been an insider – someone who has had no experience of what it is not to believe, no experience of what it is to be 'converted'. I suppose belief was the greatest gift that my parents gave me, for I was brought up in a naturally religious home where going to Church was normal and knowing one's Bible expected. Indeed this was so of the whole community, for my childhood was spent in Cornwall – certainly until well after the war cut off from 'up country' influence.

So it was that in a Cornish village church I learnt what it was to feel the presence of God – the numinous, the other, the beyond, the holy – called there by the bells from across the valley. And very early I learnt that through that experience I myself found a wholeness and togetherness which not only enabled me to be – be whom I was meant to be – but also gave me a sense of worth which was to carry me through pretty hideous days at school and beyond.

But it was not only within the Church that the reality of God was experienced, but also in the countryside of the parish: the woods and valleys, the lanes and estuaries, the rocks and ever-changing sea. Later I was to tell my pupils at both Cambridge and Oxford that I had learnt more about God through watching the sea and touching the rocks than in any number of sermons. I am not sure they always understood. Knowing where the first primroses were to be found, searching for cowries in a particular cove, noting the last swallow of the season – these were all profoundly religious experiences.

I have no doubt it was this love of the Cornish countryside and the authentic worship of its people that in part led me to the Hebrew scriptures. For there, too, one finds an unsophisticated community unafraid at revelling in the mystery of creation in all its many facets – and preserving a healthy respect for it. Hence the continued appeal of Harvest Festival to people who know that their survival is not inevitable. But the other motive was a passionate desire for justice. This I sought to fulfil in studying law and involving myself in politics. No wonder Psalmist and Prophet were to claim the bulk of my working life.

Looking back now, I can remember no overriding event which led to my ordination, no 'religious experience' to mark that whole change in my life when to the surprise of many I sought the priesthood. I was of course influenced by friends and books – especially Bonhoeffer. But what came to bear on me more and more was that unless I did take the risk and offer myself for that of which I was almost entirely ignorant, I knew I would never be my true self. And this I have found to be the main constituent of religious experience – not a blinding vision of the Divine but rather a recognition that if one is to be truly whole then there must be abandonment of all that has been before. One has to let go entirely in the sheer risk of becoming what instinctively one knows is someone more complete, though how that will be and what it will entail cannot be fathomed until the risk is taken. Here Abraham forms the pattern – going out to the unknown country, lifting the suicidal knife.

That these moments come has been my experience now on at least three occasions, all of which have dramatically altered my life, and all of which in the end I attribute to the God of surprise. And every time there has been something suicidal about the action I have had to take – a dying to live. Yet in none of these cases were there voices or visions, in none did God make himself known. The knowing was in the becoming, the recognition that the surprise had an author.

It was the study of the Bible that gave my faith content. Still after years of research and teaching I can obtain an excitement and a pleasure from the simple reading of the text. Here is all the continuous vigour of the religious experience of the ever-changing community of faith in which one finds oneself an inheritor. Of course it is not clean-cut. Much is messy and confused. Not all is as it should be. But central too is the conviction that not only does God matter to man, but man matters to God, that together God and man are on the same side and concerned with the same vision of righteousness and justice, of order and harmony both in nature and society. It has been an immense privilege to be immersed in Biblical study for so much of my life, and, far from the exercise of critical faculties weakening faith, it has constantly strengthened me in my journey, though the more I study the less luggage I carry.

But no journey would be real if there were not tensions. The whole of my ministry has been in privileged places, the whole of it surrounded by great beauty and comfort. I do not know why. It was certainly not what I envisaged when I left the lawyers' office. Nor has it dimmed my concern for justice or my interest in politics; it has simply made it all more complicated.

And there have been moments of blank despair – a passing through the deep, dark valley where the keenest emotion has been the consciousness of the absence of God. But these are sustainable because in those decisive times of risk when the decision I have taken has changed my life, when I have lifted the suicidal knife, it has been in the absence of God. Then I have had to proceed on my own and wait for confirmation later. So struggling in the tormenting darkness, one goes on knowing that only by experiencing God's absence, can one enjoy his presence again.

But mostly, of course, one is aware neither of absence nor of presence. One is simply being, getting on with the job in hand. To look for continued presence is to mistake the nature of the God who wills to know us. So it is that in the getting on with things we suddenly experience him in the unexpected and the oblique. If happily moments of wrestling are rare, so alas are moments of ecstasy. But for all the getting on with it, for all that sense of jagged inadequacy within oneself, there is yet a kind of completeness which whether in tending the garden, enjoying a gin, reading a Psalm or knowing that something however small has been achieved for someone else, assures one that the Divine is not far away.

15

Sir John Lawrence, Bt.

When I was four, or even earlier, something happened to me which has shaped the whole of my life. I am now eighty-six. We lived in Kensington Square and every afternoon I went to Kensington Gardens to play with my friend Alfred Holland, the son of the editor of the great Baron von Huegel's letters to his niece. My mother was a friend of the Baron's and also of Fr. George Tyrrel. The Baron was a lay Roman Catholic who foresaw a great many of the developments in Catholic thinking that took place in the second half of this century. He lived nearby in Vicarage Gate and he used to go into Kensington Gardens every afternoon. He made friends with all the children who came to play there and he must have paid attention to two little boys who were both the children of friends. I do not remember the Baron's face or any conversation with him. But he gave me a sense of the glory of God which never quite left me.

The Baron's work in my soul was well continued by my dear governesses Miss Monica Haslam and Miss Edith Harrington. The whole of my early childhood was filled with the glory of God. My experience was like that of Thomas Traherne but gradually 'the shades of the prison house' began to close around me. I remember once asking my mother whether everything in the Bible was true. She looked embarrassed and after a short pause said it was allegorical. I did not know what that meant and did not pursue the question.

My father was one of those blessed souls who believe without the need for any theological structure. He ultimately became a Reader in our parish church near Bath where I spent most of my childhood. He took *The Modern Churchman*, and once he even contributed to it, but he used to say with a laugh that he agreed with all the heresies, though these were often opposed to each other. One of our friends was Bishop Hensley Henson of Durham, and we children used to listen with amazement to his marvellous conversation, which could be put down in a book exactly as he said it.

So it was natural that I should go up to Durham to be confirmed in his wonderful private chapel at Bishop Auckland. He took me through the Communion Service in advance, but I had been very badly prepared for confirmation and, looking back now, I did not really understand what it was all about.

Since I had no understanding of my religion it gradually and very slowly left me, but by the time I went to Oxford I had come to an important conclusion, namely that everything in the universe was connected with everything else. So I could never understand anything to the full unless I understood everything else, which was obviously impossible. I am now convinced that this came to me from my Celtic background. This needs a little explanation.

My whole background is Irish Protestantism. My Lawrence great-great-grandfather left the north of Ireland in 1785, but our family have always married Irish girls, as it happens from the south of Ireland, and, though I live in England, I am of pure Irish blood. My brother George says that the Lawrences are like the eels who go to the Sargasso Sea for their wives. It will be objected that Irish Protestants and Irish Catholics are two distinct races, and it is true that it now suits no one's political book to say that we have anything to do with each other. But in time past we used to intermarry freely and we share so many characteristics that we are evidently of the same race. There are for instance both Catholic and Protestant O'Briens, Kennedys, MacLaughlins and MacRorys, and so on. I was brought up to think of myself as an Irish boy and I feel at home in Ireland in a special way.

The Celts were converted to Christianity very early and developed on different lines from the rest of Christendom, being before the conversion of the Anglo-Saxons virtually cut off from the rest of Europe. The religion of the Irish, the Scottish Highlands and the Welsh was rural and tribal, whereas the rest of Europe was broadly urban. After all, the word 'pagan' means a countryman. This made a difference. Celtic religion, being rural, had a different feeling for nature. It saw a kinship in all life, in the seas and the dry land. And being tribal it had a strong family feeling for members of the same clan which was without too much difficulty stretched to include all mankind. It believed that everything was interconnected.

The slow erosion of faith continued, but I would still have called myself a Christian up to the end of the war, without having a clear idea of what I meant by that. But in the end the chain snapped. For a short time I was desperately unhappy, knowing what I had lost.

I was in Dublin for Easter 1948 and went to the Good Friday service at St Patrick's Cathedral and was moved to the core. I went again on Easter Day and felt nothing at all. Nothing was proved, but on the other hand nothing was disproved. So I got out my Greek Testament and sat down quietly to read the Gospel of St Mark very slowly, a few verses every day. Before I was halfway through I was convinced that Christianity was true. But what was Christianity? What did the Church teach? So I sat down to read the early fathers of the Church and early church history. I became ecumenical and confided in Sir Kenneth Grubb, who had been my wartime chief when I was Press Attaché in the Soviet Union. He put me in touch with the Church Missionary Society of which I became an active committee member. From there on my primal vision of God returned, but of course the road was not downhill all the way.

I do not think that the present age is any wiser than its predecessors. And I see no reason why there should not be other created beings which have an influence on our lives. But if not angels, why not devils? I have no experience of angels but I have been very close to the devils. They always go away when I tell them to go in the name of the Trinity, but of course they lie in wait for me in more insidious ways.

I have enough of the eighteenth-century enlightenment in me to find it very hard to believe in intercessory prayer, though I go on trying. But a few years ago I had a stroke which at first deprived me of all speech and left me so confused that I could not pray for myself. Since then I have made a complete recovery through the prayers of others. Of course, a big factor was the love of my wife, Audrey – good medical advice. Since then I have had serious illnesses, including one in which two specialists despaired of my life, but I have made a truly remarkable recovery which is surely due to the power of prayer.

I am sure that 'God has yet more truth to break forth from his Holy Word'. It took us nearly eighteen hundred years to realise that slavery was inconsistent with Christianity, and nineteen hundred to discover that the different Churches had no business to be fighting each other, let alone to be quarrelling with other religions. In particular other religions have much to teach us, but here we must be careful. We need to 'discern the spirits'. I find no real difficulty with 'the people of a Book', the Jews and the Moslems. I think there is much to learn from the other religions, but I do not forget that some religions have taught human sacrifice and we must be on the look-out for demons. For instance, there are wonderful things to be learned from the Hindus, but there is a temple south of Madras on the way to Mahabalipuram which has something sinister and is, I am sure, an abode of devils. But, most of all, I think we can come close to God in 'primitive' religions which have kept the 'primal vision'. God has never left any generation without witnesses (Acts 14:9). But here we need particular care to 'discern the spirits'. Some primitive religions have practised human sacrifice and cannibalism.

I have never wanted to be anything but an Anglican. My soul needs a fixed liturgy, but I do not judge anyone who worships otherwise. I would love to be an Orthodox in an Orthodox country and would be Presbyterian if I could find a Church which stuck to the Book of Common Order. I could be a high-church Lutheran, or a Roman Catholic if I could find a Church that was open to other influences.

I am convinced that in Jesus Christ we have a full and perfect revelation of God, but I do not think we have yet fully grasped all the wonder that this reveals, except perhaps for a few of the greatest saints.

16

The Rev. Nicholas Stacey

It may seem paradoxical but I think I experienced the Divine most vividly through the death and destruction I witnessed in Hiroshima about eight weeks after the first atomic bomb had been dropped. I was a 17-year-old Midshipman in the Royal Navy at the time.

It was on the bright cloudless morning of 6 August 1945 at 8.15 a.m. that the bomb was dropped. First came the flash and about 100,000 died. Then came the blast and the city of over 300,000 inhabitants was virtually destroyed. This was followed by the mushroom cloud and, as one eye-witness described it to me, the living dead cried out for water, and the rubbery human faces sloughed off like masks.

When we got there even after two months, it still stank of death and decay. Most of the corpses had been disposed of – still, there were a few bones protruding from the rubble. The piteous remnants of the population squatted in a pathetic shanty-town of squalid huts tending their burns. The five miles of 'total destruction' was flat, derelict and desolate. Little groups of orphaned children picked their way around the ruins. I saw the bridge where the heat flash had roasted nine pedestrians and clearly engraved their white shadows in the roadway. There was nothing but death in Hiroshima and we were discouraged from visiting it. But it lured me as it had a macabre and ghastly fascination. I used to go off alone and clamber over the rubble, and wonder and worry. I suppose I wanted to understand it and soak in the horror of it. It had a special poignancy for us because we realised that it was probably as a result of that hell that we were alive.

Had the atomic bombs not been dropped the war would have continued for some months and we would have been involved in the forthcoming attack on some of the Pacific islands occupied by the Japanese.

Before this we had been in Hong Kong where we had retaken the island and released the prisoners of war. By the time I was eighteen I had seen suffering on the grand scale, from the destruction of Hiroshima to the poverty and hunger of Hong Kong. I wrestled about the causes of these futile wars. Why was it that people had to be roasted to death in atomic explosions and die in the gutters from starvation?

Why did pregnant Chinese women have to earn their living humping sacks of coal from junk to jetty in the heat of the midday sun? Why did thousands have to eke out an existence living in sampans? Why did alcoholic naval officers spend their evenings chasing imaginary spiders up the wardroom wall? Why was the main recreation of so many of our sailors the bars and the brothels? And if this is all there is in this life of futility – is there anything beyond?

I recalled the classical Christian teaching I had been given at my prep school and as a cadet at the Royal Naval College, Dartmouth. At the time my own, and as I now see, naive and oversimplified, interpretation and explanation of the horror and brutality of so much human existence was sin. Today, I am not quite so sure what I mean by the word. In those days hormones, heredity and environment were vague scientific terms; Freud and Marx and Einstein were little more than names to me. To an 18-year-old, the answer seemed simple: Man had misused God's precious gift of free will. He had fouled up God's good world.

Suddenly it all seemed obvious. God had sent his Son, not only to show us how to live, but to break the barriers of sin and give us the strength to live a new kind of life which would bring happiness for ourselves as well as for our neighbours. And furthermore God is not mocked; nor is He defeated. If men do not respond to his love and his call and so delay the coming of the Kingdom of God on Earth, then there is a life beyond where the inequalities of this sort will be sorted out. This explained things; it gave priorities and a programme for the present and hope for the future.

Clearly the really crucial job was not, after all, to become an Admiral, but to become a parson and to be in the front line against all evil, the fundamental cause of so much human misery; to dedicate one's life to trying to show people the possibilities, the relevance and the truth of the Christian way. The place then for me was not the bridge of the ship but the pulpit of the Church. I felt, and perhaps it was, the call of God.

My vision as a Midshipman was, I think, compounded of some real insights and some considerable conceit. Both have been dulled by the years. Neither is wholly extinguished. But in 1946 as I used to pace the broad quarterdeck of HMS *Anson* on bright Pacific nights, it all seemed so obvious, so clear and so exciting. Christ was the Hope of the World. I must sign on in His Army. I must try and offer my life to Him, to receive the strength and power that He promised and be used to bring lots of people into fellowship and communion with Him, so that together we might build a better world. I was convinced that this would be tremendously challenging, demanding and worthwhile. I think – but I am not sure – that I had a real and deep spiritual experience in those star-strung nights. Although my prayers were spasmodic and disorganised, there were many times, as there are now, when Jesus was extremely real. When I had become a Senior Midshipman I had a minute cabin – the size of a cupboard. It was many decks below. My social life during our showing-the-flag cruise around Australia after the war had ended did not make heavy demands, and I used to repair to my little cabin in the intervals between beach and cocktail parties and dances and read C.S. Lewis and other popular works of theology. I used to relive the horrors of Hiroshima and Hong Kong and, on my knees, plan things that one might do to build a better and happier world.

I have to admit that the intervening forty-five years have, at one level been a disappointing and disillusioning experience for me. This is almost certainly my fault because I hoped and expected too much from the Church. While I now see through a glass darkly I think I can still put my hand on my heart and say that I take my stand that in the end God is there. And that ultimately he has everything under control and in the long run His love will prevail. I take my stand that God revealed himself in Jesus Christ and that with this Christ men can have some kind of personal relationship through prayer. I take my stand that Christ comes to us and strengthens us in many ways and in diverse places, but most particularly I believe His spirit is with us when those who would try to follow Him break bread together in the manner of the Last Supper. I take my stand that our life here on Earth is but the beginning of something so much better which God has prepared for us which passes our understanding. And finally, I take my stand that the gates of Hell will not prevail against His Body here on Earth – which is the Church.

But for the Churches in their present form I have little hope. I do not believe they are going to be the power and influence that I had foreseen. I still see Christ at work in a number of Christians, but they are usually people who are either on the edge of the Church or who have been rejected by it. I see the Divine in the unsung priests beavering away in soulless council estates with little reward save that of knowing that they are trying to do God's will. I see more of the Divine in the presence of young people dedicated to green issues, the Third World, racial equality and services to the underprivileged than in gatherings of clergy arguing about the ordination of women and the sexual orientation of the clergy. I see very little of the Divine in bodies like the Synod of the Church of England or in Cathedral closes with their Chapters of bickering Canons. I see the Divine in the courage of young men dying of AIDS reviled by public opinion, but supported by the devotion and loyalty of their lovers.

I am nervous of those who see themselves as 'pals with Jesus', who give the impression that they have got God sewn up and are clearest about their experience of the Divine. In their certainty they often appear to express an arrogance and intolerance towards those whose experiences of the world lead them to find faith in a loving God very difficult.

But I hang on in. Most of what I understand about God has been taught to me by the Church and most of my dearest and closest friends are Christians. God may move in a mysterious way, but He is not mocked. All will be well.

17

Baroness Cox

Where children pure and happy
Pray to the blessed Child;
Where misery cries out to Thee
Son of the Mother mild;
Where Charity stands waiting
And faith hold wide the door,
The dark night wakes, the glory breaks
And Christmas comes once more.

This infrequently sung verse from the familiar carol 'O Little Town of Bethlehem' reminds us that, for the Christian, the concept of Incarnation is central to our faith and is something to be celebrated at all times and in all places, not just at Christmas time. It also reminds us that Our Lord is still coming to meet His people, to live in them and to reveal His glory through their faith and witness. It is perhaps therefore not surprising if some of the moments in my life which have been most sacramental for me, in which I have experienced God's presence and glory have been through encounters with other people whose faith shines radiantly and who show His presence in the fruits of the spirit in their lives.

I have been privileged to meet many people who have inspired me by their faith, courage and love in situations where they transform darkness into light: the darkness of suffering into healing; the darkness of repression into freedom and the darkness of despair into hope. I would like to introduce you to four of these brave people whom I have met in the course of my work with humanitarian and human rights organisations.

First, may I introduce the medical director of a hospital in Poland, and some of the mothers of children who are patients there. I have been working for Medical Aid for Poland Fund since the early 1980s.

Whenever possible, I travel on the 32-tonne trucks, partly to make sure that the aid reaches those in need; and partly to be able to return and say, 'I have been, I have seen – and this is how it really is.' So it was that I had this tragic but profoundly inspiring encounter. I was in a Children's Hospital in Southern Poland, in the cancer ward, and I was deeply dismayed to find children with leukaemia who were not being treated – not because they could not respond to treatment, but because the hospital did not have enough drugs to go round. So doctors and nurses had to select those children who would be given therapy and those who would not – and the parents were aware of the tragic predicament. I shall never forget asking them how their children coped with the suffering and one mother, speaking for all, told this true story. She said: 'Our children are very brave. We always remember the true story of a 12-year-old boy who, during the Warsaw Uprising with bombs, fires, death all around him, and his own death probably imminent, wrote these words on a wall:

> I believe in the sun, even when I cannot see it.
> I believe in love, even when I cannot feel it.

This mother and her courage, together with the courage of the other parents and children, shine like lights in the dark world of eastern and central Europe, suffering from the legacy of decades of Communist repression and trying painfully to emerge into a new era of freedom and democracy.

Another mother who also suffered under a cruel tyranny is Delia, the wife of a Romanian Baptist pastor. During the dark years of severe repression by the fearsome Securitate, she had to undergo the agony of seeing her family targeted and endangered. One day, during a birthday party she had arranged for her two little daughters, she and her husband suddenly noticed a cable attached to the drainpipe of their house and realised that the Securitate had attached a live high-voltage electric cable which would electrocute any child happening to touch the pipe. They immediately ripped it off, and were flung across the road – but no one else was hurt. Yet despite, or perhaps because of such persecution, that church flourishes like few in the secular West. I have had the honour of speaking there several times, and the tangible love which comes from the vast congregation is indescribable in its joy and its blessing.

Now, please come with me to the former USSR in September 1990, to a Human Rights Congress in what was then Leningrad. The citizens generously put us up in their own homes. I stayed with Olga and her family. Two memories will always remain with me. The first was on a morning when I tried to be helpful. I had noticed that we hardly ever ate meat; the only night we had done so, Olga and her family did not eat with us. I had a suspicion that they had given us their only meat. In an effort to be helpful, the next morning, leaving for the Congress, I asked Olga not to trouble to cook for us that evening, suggesting that just some bread and cheese would be fine. Crass Westerner that I am. Her face fell and she blushed deeply, almost whispering with embarrassment, 'But I don't have any cheese and I don't know where to get any.'

Needless to say, when I returned, there was cheese, but she had probably spent all day and a fortune getting it.

On the last night, we stayed up until 3 a.m. while Olga and her family shared their grief about their churches which had been destroyed by the Communists. They showed us a map, with blue dots for churches still standing and red dots for those which had been wilfully destroyed. The red dots outnumbered the blue dots by a vast number. Later that morning, at breakfast, Olga stood up rather shyly at the table in their small, crowded kitchen and said she wished to make a speech:

'I want to say thank you. Thank you for giving us a vision – a vision of a world where people smile. We do not have such a world. When I go to work, when our son goes to school, we cannot smile. We do not know whom we can trust. But you have given us a vision of a world where people smile and the hope that one day we can have a world like that too.'

I had to reply: 'Thank you for giving us a vision. You have given us a vision of a world where people have kept faith, hope and love alive in times of great difficulty; and I believe when God looks down from heaven you make Him much happier than we do in the West. For we in the West ought to smile – we have so much to smile about. We have our freedom and relative material abundance. But you have kept a light of faith, hope and love burning in times of great darkness – and that is a much greater vision. Thank you for giving us that vision to take back to the West.'

Finally, I felt the presence of God in the grief and love of an old man I met in a deserted village in Nagorno Karabakh, a small traditionally Armenian Christian enclave relocated by Stalin in Azerbaijan. In the summer of 1991, President Gorbachev aligned the Soviet Fourth Army with the president of Azerbaijan's fearsome 'Black Beret' or OMON forces to carry out brutal, forced deportations of the Armenians from their ancient homelands, depriving them of lands, homes, possessions and uprooting them from the villages where their ancestors have lived, died and been buried for centuries. Many atrocities were committed in the process of deportation. The Armenians subsequently fought to try to regain their homelands. In October 1991, I was visiting one of these villages on a human rights mission undertaken by Christian Solidarity International and the Andrei Sakharov Foundation. It is a beautiful village, called Buzluk, set high in the mountains, with attractive little streets, and homes which had been the pride of the villagers, in which they had invested their life's earnings. Now it is a ghost village – only the old people have returned, preferring to die in the land of their ancestors than to remain in the relative safety of exile in Armenia.

An old man was sitting on a wooden seat in the main village street. He described how the Azerbaijanis had attacked their village with tanks, helicopters and armoured personnel carriers. His son had been killed on the first day of fighting. When the victorious Azerbaijanis later entered the village they found his newly dug grave and, familiar with the Armenian custom of burying their dead in their best clothes, exhumed his son's body, taking his new suit and ripping out his gold teeth. The old man then invited us into his home which had been ransacked by the Azerbaijanis. All he had left with which to face the harsh winter was a pile of walnuts and a few apples. He insisted on giving his apples to us.

I wish to pay tribute to these brave, loving people, and to many others, who display in their lives superhuman qualities of faith in adversity, hope in tragedy, and love even under persecution. In their lives and their witness, I have experienced the power of a loving God, whose ways are not the ways of this world; a God who gives to His people His abundant grace, enabling them to witness to His redeeming love and to share with others the sacrament of His Presence.

18

The Rev. Marcus Braybrooke

At the Satcitananda ashram in South India, I began these reflections on 'Experiencing God'. It is the ashram of Father Bede Griffiths, a Christian monk who has entered deeply into Hindu spiritual traditions and has tried in his community to relate Christian and Hindu mysticism.

Why have I come? Curiosity, partly. I have long known Fr. Bede and his writings, but have not previously visited the ashram. To see and talk with Fr. Bede? – only to find he is still in America. To learn about the meeting in the spirit of Hindu and Christian? Yes, but above all in the hope of a deeper experience of the Divine.

Yet had I not experienced God in the welcome of an old friend who had waited in the heat to greet me at Madras airport – or in the affectionate farewells of my family? Should I have experienced God in the cripple on the station platform, too weary to sit up and beg?

At first the physical discomfort of sitting cross-legged on the floor, sleeping on a hard board and readapting to an Indian way of life made concentration difficult. The friendship of others at the ashram helped me to relax. Then walks beside the great holy river Cauvery at sunset and at sunrise renewed the 'sense of presence' – an awareness of the scale of the universe and my humble place in it – and a sense of peace and stillness. I felt as if I were able to relax in a warm ocean of love and that my worries and insecurity were gently washed away. I thought of my mother dying of cancer and knew that she, too, would soon be free from physical discomfort and humiliation, relaxing in the same ocean of love.

Then, at the Eucharist, which incorporated so much of the Hindu temple ritual, the celebrant called us to the communion with the words, 'Jesus invites us all to share in God's limitless love.' The sense of presence became the experience of overwhelming love and acceptance. I recognised that my moments of panic, of defensiveness and of aggressiveness came from feelings of not being able to cope. But what did it matter if God wanted to make a fool of me? I was loved without reserve – all I needed was to lean on the love of God, which is always available. I sensed that this limitless love of God embraces all people and indeed the whole of creation.

Neither experience was new. I have often sensed 'the presence' in nature, most intensely in the desert of Sinai and in the outback of Australia, but also in the beauty that surrounds us everywhere in nature. I have long known the forgiving accepting love of Jesus even if, almost as often, I forget it. The Cross has always been for me the symbol of that total accepting love of God made known in Christ – a love shown in Jesus' concern for the poor and outcast. At each communion service I have been renewed in that love which the Cross communicates.

What was new was that, beside the Cauvery river, the 'presence' of mystery in nature and the revelation in Jesus of infinite love and peace were united. And sensing that love, I felt renewed compassion for other people and for all living beings.

I want to share that experience, to repeat to others the invitation offered to me by Jesus. Yet if others have had the same invitation, from other hands, to enter into the limitless love of God, it is reason for rejoicing. I am not concerned who has the best seats in heaven.

I hope that the experience of the Divine will lift me out of relapses into selfishness and self-reliance. God is to be experienced in the kindness of friends and love of family. God is to be met in every person – although it is not easy to remember this in the bustle and begging of an Indian bus station. God may meet with us in every conversation and telephone call.

But how to communicate that sense of peace and infinite love in all the tensions and arguments and conflict of daily life and indeed in the life of the Church? Only by making myself vulnerable, being willing to absorb the pain and hostility of others, by in some small measure sharing the passion of Christ, which changes people from selfishness to self-giving. I can only do this if I am constantly renewed in the experience of God's limitless love. Only as I more fully appropriate that love will my love, like that of Jesus, know no limits and I will become an instrument of his peace.

If the river Cauvery united for me the sense of the divine presence in nature and the experience of boundless grace in the Cross of Christ, my daily life has yet to be fully united and transformed by those experiences. I long for the Holy Spirit to unite my life with God whose glory is revealed in the creation and whose love is proclaimed on the Cross.

O Holy Spirit, Lord of grace,
  Eternal fount of love,
Inflame, we pray our inmost hearts
  With fire from heaven above.

As thou in bond of love dost join
  The Father and the Son
So fill us all with mutual love,
  And knit our hearts in one.

19

Professor Sir Norman Anderson

To me the phrase 'experiencing the Divine' immediately suggests the approach of the mystic. But I am no mystic by nature, and any such tendency is scarcely encouraged by the study of law! 'The Divine', moreover, is an essentially nebulous expression. It would certainly cover, for example, the experiences claimed by members of the heterogeneous mystic or dervish Orders of Islam, almost all of which resort to some variety of the *dhikr*, or continuous repetition of some divine name or formula, to attain a state of ecstasy in which they seek a mystical communion, or even union, with Allah.

By contrast, such experience of God as I can claim comes essentially through my mind rather than my emotions, and through the Bible rather than any direct revelation. It comes from Abraham, who walked with God; from Moses, who conversed with him 'face to face'; from David, the psalmist, warrior and lover who, for all his faults, could be called 'a man after God's own heart'; and from the long line of Hebrew prophets who pointed forward to the supreme revelation of God which was to come in the person of Jesus Christ and the witness of the apostolic church. The revelation of God in the gospels and epistles of the New Testament is such, indeed, as to make me marvel how Old Testament believers could have enjoyed the personal knowledge they clearly had of the God whom I can scarcely begin to know except through the life, teaching, atoning death and triumphant resurrection of Jesus Christ our Lord.

Intellectually, the lynchpin of my faith is the solid evidence, which I find wholly convincing, for the resurrection of Jesus Christ from the dead. It is to this evidence that I would always myself go back in any crisis of faith, and to which I would point anyone else in search of intellectual conviction. As Christians it is absolutely vital that we have a *living* Saviour; but he could never have become our Saviour had he not first died the atoning death which, alone, could reconcile us with a holy God. It is only through the Cross of Calvary that I, for one, have been able to experience the wonder of God's full and free forgiveness. And I believe it is a plus, rather than a minus, that this has not come to me from any private, mystical encounter, but on the basis of facts of history and Scripture; for the forgiveness and personal acceptance to which they point have not only become my most treasured experience, but one that I can share with others.

I cannot point to any particular date on which I passed spiritually from death to life. I was brought up in a Christian home and made a positive response to the Gospel from childhood; but what Christians term 'assurance' dawned only slowly, over a period of some years. If, however, I were to be challenged – as was a missionary to Africa of whom I have read – as to when I was 'saved', I should be happy to answer, with him: 'I was saved at precisely 3 p.m. on the afternoon of the first Good Friday!'

I wish I could say that I have made steady progress in my spiritual pilgrimage, but I cannot. There have been many ups and downs in my experience. I spent four happy years as a student in Cambridge, where I did unexpectedly well in my law examinations and learnt basic lessons in prayer and Evangelism in the Cambridge Inter-collegiate Christian Union. There was a strong emphasis at that time on overseas missions, and this no doubt played a part in my growing conviction that, instead of opting for an academic career or reading for the Bar, I should go as a missionary to Egypt – following in the steps of Douglas Thornton and Temple Gairdner, whose biographies had challenged me. So I went on a visit to Egypt to see missionary work at first hand and pray for the divine guidance which I have never found easy to discern. My tentative decision to become a candidate for what was then the Egypt General Mission was, therefore, greatly strengthened by the full agreement of my fiancée, who had herself been born in Egypt. We were tempted to marry first and then offer to join the Mission, but we felt that we ought to defer to the normal discipline at that time for engaged couples that they should not marry until the wife had passed two language examinations.

I found the first nine months as a missionary particularly difficult. There was the sheer slog of Arabic study, for I am an exceedingly poor linguist; there was the curtailment of all other activities; and there were months of insomnia – caused basically, I now realise, by sheer lack of faith. Then my fiancée came to the rescue by passing two language examinations at once! So we were married at her parents' home in Alexandria and sent on short leave.

The next seven years saw the birth of our two daughters, much language study (I well remember trying to pronounce Arabic words while pushing a pram!), some varied missionary experience in Ismailia, and preparation for student work. This involved establishing a home near the University of Cairo, permission to attend lectures in Arabic literature and Islamic law, and the writing of my first book. Had this been in English it would have been entitled *Faith and Reason*; but it was in Arabic and aimed primarily at nominally Christian students who thought that Western culture had completely undermined Christian faith – and, through them, at Muslims too. Sadly, these years were marked by much failure in my walk with God.

They were terminated by the advent of the Second World War. We were on short leave in England when war was declared, and had to scuttle back to Egypt through a blacked-out France and a very wary Mediterranean. But soon the problem of divine guidance arose once more; should I, or should I not, volunteer? Had I been in charge of a mission hospital the answer would probably have been no; but I was not. I had no stomach for fighting, and had been inclined to a vague Christian pacifism; but Hitler clearly had to be stopped, and could I leave it all to others? I was ill at the time, so it was no hurried decision; but I contacted GHQ Cairo, was asked if I would serve with Arab guerrillas, and was sent to a British regiment in the desert for three weeks' weapon training. Then, quite unexpectedly, I was appointed Arab Liaison Officer of the Libyan Arab Force. This included recruiting the troops and keeping in close contact with Libyan sheikhs and members of the Sanusi mystical fraternity – especially with Sayyid Idris al-Sanusi, subsequently King of Libya. Later, I was taken over by the branch of GHQ Cairo responsible for a military form of colonial government in Cyrenaica, Tripolitania, Eritrea and the Dodecanese. So it was through no choice of my own that I never had to fire a shot in anger.

It was not until 1946 that I was able to travel home to England on release leave to become the first Warden of Tyndale House, Cambridge. Bought during the war by what is now the Universities and Colleges Christian Fellowship, only a very modest start had been made in building up what today is a splendid residential library for Biblical research. But first I myself badly needed spiritual renewal. Happily, the church we attended was soon visited by some British and African members of the Rwanda Revival, through which there had been a widespread quickening of spiritual life in East Africa and elsewhere. Their primary emphasis was that the basic secret of walking closely with God (after the initial experience of salvation through faith in the atoning death of our Lord Jesus Christ) is instantly to confess any sin or failure of which one's conscience becomes aware, and to seek, and receive, renewed forgiveness. I found this simple but searching teaching a great help.

When, in Egypt, I had accepted the post of Warden of Tyndale House I hoped I might make myself into a reasonably competent

Biblical scholar. So I enrolled in a beginners' class in Hebrew and tried to brush up my very schoolboy Greek. The latter certainly helped to enrich my early morning Quiet Times – feeding my soul on the New Testament epistles. But almost at once I was asked to give a course of lectures in the University on Islam, and subsequently to teach Islamic law in both London and Cambridge. My wife and I had originally hoped to return to the Middle East after three years; but we were unable to make any satisfactory arrangements for our daughters' holidays from boarding school, and then an unexpected, but much prized, son was added to our family. So it seemed clear that we must be based in England; that Tyndale House must have a professional Biblical scholar as Warden; and that I should accept a lectureship in Islamic law in London. This soon blossomed into a chair in Oriental Laws, subsequently combined with becoming Director of the Institute of Advanced Legal Studies.

These two posts involved much travelling and many interesting tasks, besides the writing of books and articles. But I was also able to take many opportunities to preach, talk and write about the supreme revelation of 'the Divine' – God made Man in Christ Jesus – which means more to me than anything else in life. Faith was tested when our son Hugh, who had become President of the Cambridge Union when already suffering from secondary cancer, died after four major operations. He had combined firm Christian faith with being a flaming socialist who longed to turn the world upside down. But during the night before he died, not yet twenty-two years of age, he came out of a coma to find a Christian doctor standing by his bed. 'I think it is getting near the end now, isn't it?' he asked. And when the doctor said, 'Well, Hugh, I think you are drawing near your Lord,' he replied: 'Yes, I am drawing near my Lord. I am at peace. I think my work is done.' This was a great comfort.

Further sorrows followed five years later, when our two daughters died, within three weeks of each other, in somewhat tragic circumstances. Four grand-daughters, and now six great-grandchildren, survive. But my wife, who has over the years had a lot of pain and seven operations, has now developed Alzheimer's Disease, and has to go into hospital frequently for respite care.

Inevitably, I am often asked: 'Why do Christians experience suffering?' To this question there are, I think, three primary answers. Sometimes it is divine chastisement for sin or waywardness, since 'the Lord disciplines those he loves, and he punishes everyone he accepts as a son'. Sometimes it is to teach us positive lessons, such as endurance. And sometimes it is simply a question of sharing in the calamities which befall so many people in a fallen world. Why should Christians be exempt? They have spiritual resources that others do not claim. How, otherwise, could Christians comfort those who suffer? I have no doubt that all these three answers apply to me.

As I write, I am reading Dr Martyn Lloyd-Jones's splendid exposition of Romans 8:15-17: 'For you did not receive a spirit that makes you a slave again to fear, but you received the Spirit of sonship. And by him we cry, "Abba, Father." The Spirit himself testifies with our spirit that we are God's children. Now if we are children, then we are heirs – heirs of God and co-heirs with Christ, if indeed we share in his sufferings in order that we may also share in his glory.' For me this is 'experiencing the Divine'.

20

Sir Sigmund Sternberg

On the face of it it seems a little incongruous to ask a businessman to contribute a few words on experiencing the Divine. It seems an abstract idea that ill fits a man of affairs. And yet – having been invited to make a small contribution I was in a way forced to take stock.

My Jewish orthodox religious background certainly gave me words relating to and addressing God since I was a child in Hungary. The years immediately preceding the Second World War as well as the period of its outbreak certainly gave me, like all my fellow-Jews, reason enough to pray and plead with the Almighty. It was perhaps at that stage that I first came to acknowledge that humans on their own would not be able to face what we then feared lay ahead. And when that premonition turned out to have been based on something resembling human experience, that could not begin to match the horrendous reality of the Sho'ah, questioning the Divine seemed one way to come to terms with the unspeakable.

Life carried on. Surviving members of the family were taken in. There was a great deal of rebuilding, emotional and practical, to be done. As a businessman the latter certainly filled the years of ever-increasing activity. It was inevitable that I was approached to help those less fortunate than myself. This again started the niggling question 'Why?' And with this involvement grew and awareness that there must have been some reason, some purpose, why I was permitted to survive.

I was not trained in, nor am I particularly inclined to use, the vocabulary of theology, but increasingly I came to believe that somehow I was charged with taking responsibility and using the gift of free will, so easily accessible in the country that had become home to me, to make a choice how best to involve myself in helping to bring about a better world. Again, I was fortunate. I met outstanding people in my own as well as in the Christian communities who introduced me to the work of inter-religious dialogue and I knew what I was called to do: to contribute my experience to further this work.

In a way I feel humbled by being able to serve in this way. I am not sure that I would call this experiencing the Divine. But I do believe that taking responsibility and making choices are in human terms expressions of divine will. And if that contribution of mine can in an infinitesimal way bring about a better future for my grandchildren then with God's blessing they and their children will experience a more peaceful world which to me encompasses the meaning of experiencing the Divine.

21

The Rt. Rev. Lord Blanch

I look back over seventy years or so as the youngest son of a farmer, as a schoolboy in London, as an insurance official, as a navigator in the RAF, as a student in Oxford, and then for over forty years as an ordained member of the Church of England – as a country parson, as a theological teacher, and subsequently as Bishop of Liverpool and Archbishop of York, heavily involved in ecclesiastical and public affairs. And now I am constrained by the editor to answer the question – what 'experience of the Divine' underlies this busy and varied life, largely devoted to what is understood to be 'the service of God'? I remember J.B. Phillips, a doughty translator of the Scriptures, saying once at a retreat he was conducting, 'I get very tired of religion', and then after a pause, 'but I never get tired of Christ'. Looking back over a life lived in the public service of religion, and indeed sometimes tired of it, I have to ask the question – what emerges from behind all this activity, what is it that has given meaning and significance to it all?

'Heaven lies about us in our infancy.' Insofar as I recall those early years on a farm in the Forest of Dean, they spoke to me of a beautiful countryside, of the sheepdog who was my inseparable companion, of warm days on the flagstones outside the front door, the cows, the horses, the hens and the pigs. Memory conjures up the magic of it all, the sense of a good world, sustained by a beneficent Creator. The idyll was violently interrupted by the sudden death of my father, the sale of the farm and a traumatic removal with my mother to join my older brothers in suburban London. But those early years gave me an inchoate experience of the Divine, which has never altogether left me, and has coloured my imagination ever since. There was little 'magic' about life in a London suburb, and we obviously had financial problems, though largely screened from my view. My mother, in addition to ill-health, had her anxieties about the future, when inevitably my older brothers would marry and move away. I recall a particular moment of tension in the household, which prevented me from sleeping, when I reacted in an untypical way: I got out of bed, knelt down and said the only prayer I knew – 'Our Father ...'. I heard no answering voice from heaven, but I felt better, reassured, no longer alone. I went to sleep. If the farm had given me an experience of the

Divine as the beneficent Creator, this incident gave an impression of the Divine Father, replacing the father whom I had so prematurely lost.

My early contact with the Church was of a formal kind. I attended school services with little enthusiasm, and was prevailed upon to join the choir of the local parish church with even less enthusiasm. But I had moved within the orbit of a Christian community and within sound of the gospel. I owe everything to the curate who made time to listen to my 'agnostic' burblings and was prepared to tolerate my youthful posturing. When I joined the RAF in 1940 I took with me a book of daily Bible readings which he had given me, and took with me, too, the memory of a godly man of prayer who epitomised everything in my innermost being of what I longed to be. No one who has not experienced it can imagine the shock of being uprooted from home and being plunged into barrack-room life, with its seemingly meaningless rituals and its rough companionship. But I was sustained by, and found space and time for, daily prayer for the first time in my life. It was distinctly not an 'experience of the Divine' but it exposed possibilities which could lead to such an experience. And so it proved to be. Many months later I found myself on a transit camp near Manchester, awaiting an overseas posting. It was my misfortune, as I supposed, to be put in charge of the camp guard over the Christmas period, while everyone else went home. I had a Nissen hut to myself and nothing to do for a whole week. It was an unsought opportunity to read the gospels seriously for the first time in my life. I subscribed to no theory of biblical inspiration, I brought with me no formal Christian education. I was not aware even why I was reading the gospel at all. Yet the experience changed my life. I suppose that if I had attempted to put it into words it would have been – 'If this is not true then nothing is true.' From that time my emotions, my thoughts, my aspirations were centred on that man of Nazareth recorded in Holy Scripture. I tremble now to think what would have happened to me if God in His divine providence had not confined me to camp that Christmas. It was an experience of the Divine mediated to me through the Holy Scriptures which as yet I had no reason to venerate.

'When Providence puts a good book in my way I bow to its decree and purchase it as an act of piety.' If the Station Warrant Officer, in drawing up the guard list, had been the unwitting tool of Providence, it was a book which took me on to the next stage. My wife-to-be and I, separated as we were by some 200 miles, saw it reviewed in the same newspaper and both bought a copy. It was called *Midnight Hour*. It conveyed the message of a highly gifted and articulate man who had struggled over a period of months with the same issues which at a lower level of comprehension had surfaced in my own life. It was a book which presented the starkness of the choice between what life might offer and what Christ demanded. I had to make my choice on the basis of a much more restricted experience and without the author's intellectual capabilities. Every 'seeker' needs his 'prophet' if he is to be alerted to the demands of the Eternal. And he needs his everyday companion in the faith too. My own marriage has been an experience of the Divine in the sense that we have had to wrestle with the mundane problems of bringing up a large family on limited means, we have had to face the tension between my professional life as a clergyman and the due regard for the children committed to our care. We have had to learn how to balance constant exposure to the public with the need for an intimate and private life in the home. This is not the stuff that dreams are made of: it has been the struggle to maintain and to respond to the experience of the Divine amidst the ordinary and inescapable decisions which press upon any marriage.

Even more remarkable in the providence of God than the Station Warrant Officer's decision to put me on the guard for Christmas, and the publication at the same time of a book which chimed with my own experience, was an event which took place when I was briefly stationed near Perth in Scotland. I had planned to see a film in the local cinema, but when I arrived I discovered to my annoyance that the film was showing later than I expected and would not be over in time for me to get back into camp. So by an impulse which I cannot now explain I determined to call on the Bishop of St Andrew's, whose official residence was in Perth. So I presented myself on his doorstep, unannounced, and asked whether I could see him. He could not have been more friendly as I discussed with him what I might do after the war, given my recent experience of the Christ whom I had encountered in the Scriptures. He obviously saw within me the possibility of ordination and offered to send my name to what later became the Church's Advisory Council for the Training of the Ministry. He prayed with me and I accompanied him to Evensong. I did not resent having missed the film. It was a crucial step and I owe it to a gracious man of God who found time to talk to a brash young airman, who had little notion of what he wished to talk about.

Of my 'experience of the Divine' in the life of the Church I have to speak with a certain ambivalence. I owed my faith in the first instance to a faithful minister of the Church, and no doubt my mind was subtly influenced by my experience of the church choir, the church music and the church building. But I was not enamoured with the Church, and the RAF Chaplains I encountered in the course of my service must have been puzzled by this ambivalence. I could have echoed that seemingly cynical though perceptive remark 'The Church must be of God, because otherwise nothing so bad could have lasted so long'. But I had glimpses of what a fellowship of Christians could accomplish even within the narrow boundaries of service life. I recall a certain 'renewal' experience at Cranwell. Out of the ground, as it seemed, with little in the way of organisation to encourage it, there sprang little groups of men who met informally in the canteen or the barrack room to study the Bible. It perceptibly altered the attitude to the Christian faith of many others in the unit. For me it was an example of the 'seed growing secretly' in the soil and bearing fruit without the benefit of formal organisation or ecclesiastical initiation. We were a fellowship drawn together, as I would have to believe, by the Holy Spirit, and rewarded with a certain experience of the Divine.

Perhaps as a result of this experience in Cranwell I did not react all that enthusiastically to the suggestion that I might be ordained after the war. I did not relish an official association with what seemed to me then a large, lumbering institution, with which at that time I had little sympathy. That, despite my misgivings, I was ultimately ordained I can only attribute to a chain of circumstance over which I had little control. I attended, with some reservations, the first selection conference ever held in the Church of England. It was for service personnel only, and it was held in Calcutta when I was serving as a navigator in South East Asia Command. When I got back to England after demobilisation I discovered that I had been recommended for training. By this time I was married with no visible means of support. But a higher authority had ordained that returning servicemen who had shown themselves capable of earning a higher salary than they had been earning as civilians 'showed promise' and could apply for grants towards higher education. My academic qualifications were slight, but I had read Classics at school. I had the necessary entry qualifications and I was awarded a place at Oxford to begin my studies for the ministry. Circumstance is not a dramatic, evidential sign of the divine will, but it was an impressive and encouraging aid. I bowed to divine decree.

I have sometimes had to warn would-be ordinands that ordination is not a first-class ticket to heaven. It does not necessarily produce a heightened experience of the Divine. Devotion will glow only intermittently under the pressure of repeated public services. Listening for the personal word of God in the Bible may be made more difficult by the incessant demand for talks, sermons and lectures. The everyday experiences which accompany any pastoral charge in the parish, the college or the diocese, often serve as grim reminders of the hardness of men's hearts and the painful mysteries of life. Ministry to others may prove to be a rapid and disagreeable course in self-discovery. Disdainful public attitudes towards the Church as an institution can easily sap the morale of those who are committed to lifetime service within it. But it remains true that there are countless ministers who serve sacrificially and without visible reward to whom the 'disdainful' public still turn for comfort and consolation in the darker moments of life. There are those who preach and live the gospel in forbidding inner-city parishes and remote, unrewarding country areas without the satisfaction of visible response. But on the day of judgement long-forgotten figures from the past will rise up and call them blessed, testifying to an experience of the Divine in their own lives as the result of a personal ministry to them, however casual and ineffective it seemed at the time. Moses could well be regarded as the prototype of any minister of God. He struggled incessantly to convey to a perverse and hard-hearted nation something of his own experience of the Divine. Some of them and certainly some of their children did in the end cross the Jordan into their promised land. My experience of the Divine, fragmentary and elusive as it is, has been a lifelong progress from a wholly misplaced self-confidence to a faltering trust in the God and Father of our Lord Jesus Christ:

> Let me no more my comfort draw
> From my frail hold of Thee
> In this alone rejoice with awe
> Thy mighty grasp of me.

22

The Very Rev. John Simpson

As the existence of God is ultimately a matter of faith, so claims to have experienced God fall into the same category of faith. Claims to know God, to have encountered God, to have a relationship with God – such claims are not susceptible of proof, and yet the conviction and the testimony of the adherents of nearly all the major world religions are that God can be sought and found, and that discovery of God transforms existence.

The Christian tradition lays down no one way of experiencing God. Indeed, the Christian conviction that the initiative in an encounter with God lies with God and not with the man or woman who may claim to have such an encounter means that any situation may be the means of encounter, and this is borne out in Christian experience. However, from earliest times, worship has been seen as the activity which so frequently can open up an experience of God. In I Corinthians 14, St Paul, in discussing the very complex worship activities of the congregation of Christians at Corinth during their weekly assembly, does so on the assumption that through what they are doing, they are experiencing God, and that this is something obvious and with powerful impact – so powerful, indeed, that even an unbeliever appreciates it and is affected by it. He makes the assertion:

> If all prophesy, and an unbeliever or outsider enters, he is convicted by all, he is called to account by all, the secrets of his heart are disclosed; and so, falling on his face, he will worship God and declare that God is really among you.

To describe encounter with God as a church service may strike many today as a little unreal, since we all know that a church service can be dull and boring and depressing. But sometimes a church service can be a confrontation with God, and the fact that many do not appreciate this says more about the inner state of such people than about the God who is prepared to meet them. I well remember preaching some time ago at a small village in Kent. The procession of servers and clergy entered, moved halfway along the central aisle and stopped. No one seemed afraid of the silence which followed, or to be embarrassed by it, but as the silence progressed and deepened, a great sense of wonder seemed to spread through the congregation: wonder at approaching the God who actually meets us.

The experience of a sense of wonder, combined with a growing reverence and an appreciation of personal littleness, so frequently occurs in attempts which Christians make to describe their individual experience of God. I shall not forget the sense of awe, wonder, even praise, which was my response as, for hours, I wandered through the great Picasso Exhibition of 1961, at the Tate Gallery. I am convinced that this was not just appreciation of, or joy in a particular form of art, which I confuse with awe and wonder and praise of God. It was in a real way experience of God. It was the sort of thing that Christians mean when they say that we live in a sacramental universe. The world, whether it is the elements, the forms of nature, man with all his abilities and skills – all is 'charged with the grandeur of God', and sometimes this breaks through with such brilliance that we cannot miss it. Millions will echo this experience, but for the Christian, what we do in church – that is, in our specific acts of worship – should heighten our awareness of this, our sensitivity to this, so that we begin to see God in more and more. Which is why, in our acts of worship, poetry, music, silence, colour, movement are of such importance, for these heighten our awareness.

But the experience of God in the majestic and beautiful is not all. At the very heart of Christianity, there is the glory of God revealed through the cross and death of Jesus Christ, and here we come to what is, for most people, hardest to accept – the experience of God in all that is death-dealing in this world. In essence, this is seeing through the evil, cruelty and destructiveness of the world, to the greater reality of God's glory, the transforming, life-giving power of his love. Put in a different way, in terms of Jesus Christ, it is seeing the crucifixion in the light of Easter Day. In the crucifixion of Jesus Christ, there is the portrayal of evil in all its reality and god-forsakenness. But on the third day, he rose again, and in the light of the resurrection, the evil of Good Friday is seen to be transformed by something infinitely more real, the life-giving love of God. The acceptance of the reality of evil, suffering and death becomes a means for the experience of God, provided that these things are seen in the light of the ultimate, final and most real reality of all, the reality of God's love, which Easter declares is ultimately victorious over everything which opposes it.

Here again, what is done in church, in the Christian Eucharist, heightens awareness of this, and sensitivity to this, and experience of this. For what we do with bread and wine takes us to the heart of God and his torn world, and at the same time, to his victory and re-creation of mankind and the world in glory.

Though not the only means to the experiencing of God, the Christian Eucharist is the promised way to that experience.

23

Professor Erich Segal

I have always believed that the most extreme expressions of faith are born of despair, when the mind is overwhelmed by truth and the soul by a desire for the impossible.

The most obvious instance is when a loved one is terminally ill. People have even been known to seek spiritual aid from priests of other faiths. Again, atavistically, they endeavour to ascribe some external source to make their misfortune *comprehensible*.

This is the case in the myth of the *dybbuk* – which appears not only in Jewish literature but even in the New Testament (as an 'unclean spirit'). The etymology of the word comes from the Hebrew root 'to cleave', the notion being that the demon enters the body of the person, usually as a punishment for some misdeed, and occupies it with adamantine strength.

The *Encyclopaedia Judaica* has an enlightening article on the role of the *dybbuk* among Jewish mystics. Perhaps the most important of them was one of the many rabbis of the Luria dynasty (hence the name of my fictional characters) who conceived of methods to exorcise evil spirits from those afflicted.

The most famous literary version of this phenomenon is the play *The Dybbuk* by S. An-ski (1916). The story has also been novelised by Romain Gary and set to music for at least three operas. My most personal contact with this seemingly irrational – even pagan – rite of exorcism was in Paddy Chayefsky's brilliant play *The Tenth Man* (1959) which equated the *dybbuk* with psychopathological forces in ourselves.

I also recollect that as a child I had many a nightmare after seeing the classic Habimah Players perform An-ski's drama when they were visiting New York.

Acts of Faith, the novel from which the following excerpt is taken, was the most controversial book I have ever written, raising hackles among the conservative extremes of both Catholicism and Orthodox Judaism. Yet mine was a plea for tolerance and the realistic confrontation of the problems I believe God has placed before us to solve on our own. The possession of the sin draws much on my childhood memories, the message is the one I finally achieved as an adult.

*

We got to the synagogue at about one-thirty in the morning. It was dark except for the lights in front near the Holy Ark.

Half a dozen men were gathered in a circle around my father, who was seated, wringing his hands. Among them were my Uncle Saul, my brother-in-law Dovid – a *yeshiva* teacher who was married to my older half-sister Malka – and Rena's husband Avrom, pale and quivering.

Reb Isaacs, the sexton, was scurrying back and forth between them and a far corner where the women – my half-sister and my mother – were taking turns trying to soothe Rena, who was groaning unintelligibly.

Dr Cohen, obviously with Papa's dispensation, stood in the segregated women's section and shrugged his shoulders.

As we drew nearer, I suddenly realised that Beller did not have a skullcap. Luckily I always carry a spare, which I offered to him, half-afraid he would refuse to wear it. He simply nodded and placed it on his head.

As we joined the men, I saw a bizarre figure hovering close to my father – a wizened, bearded old man in a long caftan and wide-brimmed hat. He seemed to be whispering to all present, punctuating his words with emphatic gesticulations.

Standing respectfully a few paces behind him was a tall, cadaverous youth, obviously some kind of assistant.

At this moment, Father saw us. His face was gray as a tombstone. In all my life I had never seen him so distressed. His shirt collar was open and his prayer shawl draped over a wrinkled jacket. He hastened toward us and motioned me aside.

'Danny,' he confided hoarsely, 'I'm glad you're here. I really need your support.'

Him need *me*? That was an unsettling reversal of roles.

When I asked who the strange old man was, he looked at me with pain and helplessness.

'He's Rebbe Gershon from the Williamsburg *Talmidey Kabbala*. I asked him to come. You know that our ancestors were mystics, but I myself never believed in this sort of black magic. And now it's right in front of my eyes.'

He paused and added mournfully, 'What else could I do? Anyway, we have another problem. We don't have ten men. I could only ask people we could trust. So there's Rebbe Saul, the two sons-in-law, Reb Isaacs, Rebbe Gershon and his apprentice, Dr Cohen – and now you make the ninth. We still need one more.'

He looked at my companion and asked, 'Is this gentleman – ?'

'This is Professor Beller. Papa ...' I interrupted.

'Oh,' my father responded. 'Are you Jewish, Professor?'

'I'm an atheist,' he replied. 'Why don't you ask one of those women to make the quorum?'

Father ignored him and demanded urgently, 'Will you just stand with us? That's all the Law requires.'

'Very well,' Beller conceded.

A sudden piercing shriek came from the front of the synagogue and echoed from the rafters.

The men had now moved Rena to the front of the pulpit and surrounded her. This time, despite the hysteria in her voice, I could hear the words. 'I am Chava Luria, and I cannot be admitted into the life of the world-to-come until the man who murdered me does penance.'

Beller and I exchanged glances.

'Does that sound like your sister?' he asked.

'No,' I answered, my heart pounding. 'I've never heard that voice before in my life.'

As we neared the circle, I could see Rena writhing on a chair, her face contorted. She had pulled off her *sheitel* and looked so grotesque I could barely recognise her. Her heavy-jowled husband, Avrom, stood by her, looking helpless and terrified.

I went to her, bent down, and said as gently as I could, 'It's me. Danny. Tell me what's wrong.'

She moved her lips and yet another unearthly sound emerged. 'I am Chava. I have attached myself to Rena's soul, and I will remain until I have revenge.'

I froze. Like the other onlookers, I was petrified.

Only Beller reacted. To Rebbe Gershon's visible annoyance, he stepped forward, knelt next to my sister, and simply spoke to the voice as if conversing with my father's long-dead wife.

'Chava,' he said quietly, 'I'm Dr Beller. What is this revenge you're talking about? Who do you think has wronged you?'

The reply spewed out like lava from a volcano. 'He *killed* me. Rav Moses Luria killed me!'

Nine pairs of eyes suddenly fixed on Papa, as Professor Beller turned to him and asked, 'Do you have any idea what she's talking about?'

My father shook his head emphatically, and added in a whisper, 'I never did anything to hurt her.'

'You killed me,' howled the voice. 'You let me die.'

'No, Chava, no,' my father protested. 'I begged the doctors to do everything to save you.'

'But you made them wait. You wanted to have your son ...'

'No!' Father's face had gone chalk white.

'You have my blood on your hands, Rav Moses Luria.'

My father lowered his head to avoid the startled gazes of the onlookers and murmured in agony, 'It's not true. It's not true.' He then addressed the exorcist in suppliant tones. 'What shall we do, Rebbe Gershon?'

'Open up the Holy Ark and we will pray to chase this evil spirit out of your daughter.'

I bounded onto the pulpit, opened the doors, and pulled apart the curtains. There, row by row, stood the sacred scrolls, clothed in their gold-fringed silk and crowned with silver ornaments. They seemed to shine more brightly than ever on this night of supernatural blackness.

Rebbe Gershon turned to the others. 'We will surround this woman and recite the Ninety-first Psalm.'

We quickly turned to the appropriate page, and awaited his instructions.

He signalled us to begin.

Normally, our prayers were torrents of words moving at different speeds across the text, creating a sacred cacophony. But this time we all spoke in unison, as if the Lord had sent a metronome into our midst.

We had studied this psalm in one of my classes, where we learned that in ancient times superstitious Jews regarded it as having anti-demonic powers, since its first two verses invoke God by four completely different names.

> Oh thou that dwellest in the covert of the Most High,
> And abidest in the shadow of the Almighty;
> I will say of the Lord, who is my refuge and my fortress,
> My God, in whom I trust,
> That He will deliver thee ...

I looked over my shoulder and saw my mother and half-sister praying intensely. I glanced at all the frightened faces of the worshippers – except my father's. I could not bear to look at him.

As we recited, Rena's head slumped forward. She shook as if locked in mortal combat with the spirit who had captured her. Then suddenly she fell into a faint. Professor Beller dropped down beside her and began to take her pulse.

We all ceased praying. There was total silence. I could hear the angry winds blowing outside.

My father asked anxiously, 'Are you all right now, Rena?'

His daughter looked up, eyes pleading. From within, the demon howled once again, 'I will never leave until you beg forgiveness from the Almighty!'

Papa had his head in his hands, lost for what to do. I wanted to go to him, to comfort him. But before I could move to his side Rebbe Gershon commanded him, 'Rav Luria, you must confess.'

Father stared at him. 'But it isn't true!'

'I beg of you, Rav Luria. Do not question the Lord of the Universe. If He finds you guilty, then you must confess.'

Papa was adamant. 'But I told the doctors that *her* life was more important. You know I would have – it's the law of our religion. I am innocent!'

After a dreadful silence, once again Rebbe Gershon murmured, 'We sometimes do not realise what we do. But He who sits on High can only be placated if we ask forgiveness for the sins we might have committed.'

'All right!' my father shouted.

He sank to his knees before the Holy Ark and, sobbing, chanted the *Al chet*, the 'Great Confession of Sins', which we recite nine times on the Day of Atonement.

Without a sign or signal, all of us said in unison the congregational response to the prayer, 'Forgive us, have mercy on us, pardon us.'

When our voices finally ceased to echo in the empty synagogue, my professor spoke.

'Rav Luria, I think your daughter should be seen by a psychiatrist as soon as possible.'

Father's head snapped up. He riveted Beller with his eyes. 'You keep out of this.'

'All right, have it your way – for the time being. But remember, as a doctor I have the authority to insist that she be taken to a hospital.'

The others in the *minyan* glared at him. They would, I'm sure, have chased him out had we not needed him as a tenth man. Then they all turned to my father.

'What should we do, Rav Luria?' one of them inquired.

'Ask Rebbe Gershon,' Father answered weakly. He had clearly abdicated all authority.

'There's no alternative,' the elderly rabbi declared. 'We must perform the entire ceremony of excommunication – rams' horns, Torahs, lights – everything. These are dire circumstances and one must take the ultimate measures. Are you in agreement, Rav Luria?'

'Just tell me what you need,' Father said softly.

'First, we all put on *kittels*.' The exorcist motioned impatiently to his assistant. 'Ephraim – quickly.'

The young man rummaged through a large suitcase, and withdrew the white garments Jews wear on Holy Days – and as a burial shroud.

Rebbe Gershon turned back to my father. 'We will use seven rams' horns and seven black candles.'

'Black candles?' said my father in disbelief.

'I brought everything,' Rebbe Gershon murmured. 'I left the bag in your office.'

Papa nodded. 'Danny, hurry and get it – please.'

I charged up the stairs and entered the little office on the second floor. It looked as though it had been vandalised. Open books strewn everywhere. Tracts on mysticism and demonology. Several on the mystical theories of the sixteenth-century 'Divine Rabbi', Isaac Luria. I never knew he had such works. Or perhaps the exorcist had brought them.

Near the desk was Rebbe Gershon's weathered valise. I stared at it for a moment, frightened by what else it might possibly contain, then picked it up and carried it gingerly down the stairs.

By the time I returned to the synagogue, the others, including Professor Beller, had put on the white shrouds.

The moment I gave the bag to Rebbe Gershon, my father pushed a *kittel* at me.

'Hurry, Danny ... Let's get this over with.'

As I quickly dressed, I could hear Rena – or was it Chava? – moaning incoherently.

Rebbe Gershon now ordered seven of the men to take down Torahs from the Holy Ark. He then opened the valise and motioned me toward him.

'Here, boy, give these out.'

One by one he handed to me seven of those sinister candles.

Father was pacing back and forth, every so often slapping his forehead as if it had been stabbed with needles.

Mama nervously approached the exorcist.

'Rebbe Gershon, we want to do something. May we at least hold candles? I mean, in the women's section of course.'

The old man waved her off. Then he pointed again to me. I understood without the need of words that he was commanding me to extinguish the other lights.

In a moment the vast synagogue was drowned in darkness, except for seven candle flames.

By their eerie flickering light, the exorcist then distributed among us seven rams' horns. I took one, but I wasn't sure I could produce a sound because my lips were numb.

At another of Rebbe Gershon's signals, we again surrounded Rena, still sitting, her shoulders hunched and eyes tightly closed.

He took a deep breath, stood in front of her, and declaimed, 'Evil spirit, since you will not hear our prayer, we invoke the power of the Most High to expel you.'

And then he commanded us, 'Blow *tekiah*.'

I had always been chilled by the sound of a single ram's horn on the High Holy Days. I imagined the great blast to be the seal of God's supreme Judgement. But the sound of *seven* all at once was beyond description.

All eyes were fixed on Rena's face. She began to writhe again, and a voice clamoured from within her, 'Let go! Stop dragging me! I will not leave!' Rena seemed to surrender. She fell back in her chair, completely limp.

Rebbe Gershon persisted, beads of sweat on his brow glowing in the candlelight.

'Since you will not heed the higher spirits, I now invoke the cruelest powers of the universe to tear you out.'

He turned again to us and commanded, 'Blow *shevarim*.'

Three low, even notes came forth and filled the empty synagogue. We all bent closer to Rena. The demon was still within her, but noticeably weaker.

'All the powers of the universe are now against me,' it wailed. 'I am torn by spirits with no mercy – but despite the pain, I will not go!'

Rebbe Gershon now ordered brusquely, 'Put the Torahs back and close the Ark.'

The men obeyed as quickly as they could and, I am sure, wondered as I did what more the exorcist could do.

When we all once again encircled the *dybbuk*, the old man walked into the middle, looked straight at Rena, and roared like a lion: 'Rise up, O Lord! Let thine enemies be dispersed and scattered ... I, Gershon ben Jacov, do sunder every thread that binds you to the body of this woman.'

He paused, and then cried even louder, '*You are excommunicated by the Lord Almighty*!'

Signalling the horns again, he told us, '*Teruah*.'

Driven by blind fear, we trumpeted a sound that transformed the atmosphere into primal chaos. Though we were nearly out of breath, he urged us to keep on blowing. Now the writhing of my sister's body was so violent, it almost lifted her about the chair.

Then, suddenly, she collapsed, unconscious.

Rebbe Gershon waved at us to stop. Papa was the first at her side. He lifted her face.

'Oh, Rena, my little girl, are you all right?'

She opened her eyes slightly, but said nothing.

'Talk to me, please, my child,' he implored.

She was silent, her eyes unfocused.

Someone tapped me lightly on the shoulder. I turned. It was Beller. 'Go to her,' he whispered.

I nodded and took two or three steps towards my sister. By some miracle, she seemed to recognise me.

'Danny,' she muttered. 'Where am I? What's happening?'

'Everything's all right,' I tried to reassure her. 'Your husband's here ...'

I motioned to Avrom. He came forward, leaned down, and embraced his wife.

Reb Isaacs had put the lights back on as Rebbe Gershon's assistant collected our extinguished candles.

Following his lead, the men took off their white garments, returning to their earthly clothing.

Beller was again checking Rena's pulse, and having borrowed a penlight from Dr Cohen, was looking into her eyes. He stood up, evidently satisfied.

'Get her into bed and see she gets a lot of rest. I'm going to make sure somebody from the hospital comes to see her.'

I waited for my father to object, but he said nothing. To my astonishment, he had also become Beller's patient.

'May I speak to you for a moment, Rav Luria?' he asked.

Papa merely nodded and walked a few steps away with the professor. They had a whispered dialogue, which I could not hear. For a moment they nodded at one another, then Papa returned to the rest of us.

Avrom had his arms around Rena. I was touched by his devotion.

Then Father addressed us all. 'As you can see, the Lord of the Universe had heard our prayers. Thank you, Rebbe Gershon – and everybody.' He added with surprising severity, 'But I command you all to keep silent about what you have seen and heard tonight.'

24

The Very Rev. Wesley Carr

Throughout history the religious experience of the religious professional has been scrutinised. Claims are received with distrust: 'He would say that, wouldn't he?' Christian ministers in particular are all too aware of the strictures which Jesus placed on scribes and priests. To be a 'whited sepulchre' is not very desirable. When the minister is the dean of a Cathedral, the questions become acute. For a Cathedral represents more than the Christian faith. Many people other than worshippers lay claim to it. It offers a range of options to do with history, aesthetics, power and anonymity. Perhaps the best image of all this is that of space. Symbolised by the size of the building, the life, worship and work of a Cathedral provides all sorts of people with usable space in a pressured world. Cathedrals are inevitably ambiguous institutions, both sacred and secular, Christian and more generally religious.

I have spent nearly all of my ministry in great parish churches or cathedrals. It is a chicken-and-egg question as to why. Is it because of something in me that seeks out such places? Or is it something about these places that needs whatever I have to offer? Whatever the reason, experiencing the Divine for me is inevitably informed by the basic ambiguity of cathedrals and churches.

You cannot separate religious experience from common human experience. 'Common' describes those aspects of life that we all experience. At one level there are the great human experiences – birth, growth, transitions and ultimately death, although this is experienced only through that of others. At another there are the thousands of bits and pieces which constitute life. Whether there is always a divine dimension or component to such experience is unclear. I increasingly think that there is. And this is more often than not confirmed in conversation with others, especially those who do not profess any religious belief.

We like to think that somehow religious experience is our personal possession. But in fact it is configured by the way in which we ourselves have come to be. Three factors have been and remain important in shaping my own senses of the Divine. First, I was nurtured in the Christian faith. Everyone is brought up to believe something, even if it is not to believe. Equally, as we mature we test that upbringing and make something of it. But whatever our origins, the essential 'What if?' of religion is located there. What if my home had been different? What if I had made different decisions? What if I had not met that person? What if I had not heard that sermon? These are the hypotheses of life which generate questions of meaning, the religious dimension to all experience. They have early origins and persist with us throughout our life.

Secondly, I have had a privileged life of learning. A scholarship boy at a time when you could move through universities, I have had my mind stimulated by a series of able teachers. This side to life now feels increasingly important. The irrational dimensions to religious experience are being strongly affirmed in today's churches. By contrast I feel the demand for an apologetic which will not discount claims to experience but will not be limited to them.

This connects with the third influence. For many years I have studied unconscious behaviour in groups. Colleagues in this exploration are of many faiths and none. This, contrary to what might be expected, has not lessened the sense of the importance of religion or the pervasiveness of something beyond. On the contrary, it has confirmed to me its centrality in all human experience.

What does this imply in practice about experiencing the Divine? Putting together the contexts in which I have lived most of my life – churches and cathedrals – and the issues with which I have dealt – origins, study and the unconscious – I come to the crux where this happens. It is where we hold together our inner and our outside worlds. Obviously the two connect in many ways. It is a mark of the end of this century that people are more alert to the topic. But in our experience they also seem frequently to divide. Religious language for this complexity is that of immanence and transcendence, both of which are needed in any experiencing of what we might call God.

An essential component of any experience which we may call religious is something (or someone) beyond. The Freudian suggestion that this is merely a delusion does not hold. That dismissal has proved casual and inaccurate. But religious experience does lie in the area of illusion, where fantasy, art, religion and imagination all operate. People often have false expectations of this transcendent. They look to it as if it were something whole. We long for completion, so the argument runs, and seek it in that which lies beyond.

My experience, however, contradicts this. One consequence of working in a great institution like a cathedral is that you learn the importance of the small matter or the apparently insignificant issue.

The wealth of opportunities for all sorts of experience becomes overwhelming. So people cling to such bits or fragments as they can. 'A beautiful cathedral,' said one visitor to Bristol Cathedral. 'Thank you for the excellent lavatories.' Every preacher is familiar with the effusive thanks for helpful words which were never spoken. The experience of transcendence comes not so much through being taken out of oneself as of having the minutiae of life momentarily irradiated with the unexpected.

Over the years the particles of life inevitably accumulate and feel even more fragmented. Consequently some way of affirming them becomes all the more pressing. One major means is worship. The big event of Sunday or a special occasion is important. But the routine of the daily office is possibly even more critical. With our intense desire today to know for certain what we are doing in every facet of our life, we are in danger of destroying what worship is about. If we believe, as at least Judaism, Islam and Christianity teach, that to meet God involves risk, then such encounters cannot be casual. Nor can they be sustained. In other words, any rendezvous with God is necessarily fragmentary and unsustainable. In worship, therefore, a structure is offered us not for full-scale major meeting with God but for the momentary trysts which make up religious experience. Our minds should wander, otherwise the imagination will not work. Our wills should vacillate, otherwise we will be wary of doing anything. And our hearts should be both overwhelmed and underwhelmed with love for God, otherwise we shall use up all this energy in formal worship alone.

Such sense of God as I know is like this. The experience is fragmentary and momentary. It then follows that it is also likely to be indirect rather than direct. Religious people often hope for direct connections between what they do and what they achieve. If we pray, then something identifiable should happen. If we sing, some associated experience should occur. If we listen, we should hear what the preacher is saying. If we read, we shall understand what the Bible means. But if any of these are claimed as distinctively religious experience, it seems to me to make it false to common human experience. There is a basically tangential quality to the way we experience things in life. Connections are indirect. So when it is claimed that religious experience is not like this, I am unclear what we are discussing.

One way I find helpful in articulating the rich dimensions of the sense of God without divorcing them from the realities of life is to think in terms of verbs. In any language verbs are the active words. They are flexible. Yet great linguistic edifices are built on them. Grammarians discern three moods: indicative, subjunctive and optative. The indicative mood states what is. It is the language of conviction and creeds. There are many problems with such statements. But the believer can make them within the context of belief. They are like the pillars which hold up a cathedral. Functional, they are also fascinating in their own right. Often they are very beautiful and elegant. But they are also basic. Without them, however, there would be no cathedral. Similarly without some faith statements, religious experience could not be communicated. And that which cannot be communicated is not much use, if it exists at all.

The subjunctive mood is the mode of questioning and exploring. The form is 'Might I?' or 'Might you?'. This is the language of hypothesis. It derives from our deepest origins. If there is such a thing as innate religion, this is its material. On our cathedral analogy it is the space of the building. This is vast. It continually pulls us out of ourselves and invites our minds to wander and our imaginations to run riot. The pillars will keep the building up. But without the exploring, there is little point in there being a cathedral at all. So with religious experience, unless it consistently moves to and through the unknown, it atrophies. This is, for example, the context of prayer. My experience of prayer is that it is mostly a matter of constructing hypotheses with God. What if part of the world were like such and such? If so, what then follows to be done or believed? What if this bit of my life were changed in that way? What if things were not just what they seem? Meditation, contemplation and intercession in their different ways are all part of this process. It is the core of those moments of focused religious experience.

Finally, there is the optative mood: 'O that this were so!' There is a necessary longing in religion. Without it the practice of faith becomes a restriction rather than an inspiration. We have a wishing side to our religious experience. In our cathedral it is like sunlight bursting through the stained glass. For a moment we glimpse a rare and ethereal beauty. It is not in the light alone. It is made up of the interplay of pillars, space and light. It cannot and does not last. But irrationally, not thinking but rightly responding, we instinctively hope that it might become a permanent state. For the moment we forget that this glory lies in the way it suddenly captures our vision. The reality of religious experience is that there is no optative without the indicative and subjunctive, the staples of religion.

This joining of language to cathedral may not communicate well. It may be too personal. For me, however, it is helpful. Is this because of who I am, my inner self? Or is it simply because of where I have been fortunate to be, churches and cathedrals? Who can know? And who could decide? But this ambiguous mix of outside and inside, the transcendent and the immanent, the material and the personal, seems to me the essence of whatever it is that we mean by experience of the Divine. Its richness does not satisfy. But it still invites me onwards.

25

Lord Grimond

I have had no personal experience of the Divine. Through no Pauline conversion have I had any personal message from God. My life has not been irradiated or punctuated by glimpses of heaven. I am not aware of being the repository of any divine wisdom, nor can I point with certainty to any immediate answer to prayer. In fact I have no qualifications for contributing to this book. My faith would be much more certain had I any direct, personal experience of God.

I resemble a large proportion of mankind in calling myself a Christian but acknowledging that I am a wavering candle. I cannot point to either experience or reason for a convincing explanation of my faith. Indeed in some ways my behaviour towards religion is based on contradictions.

My prime reason for clinging to some Christian belief is that I was brought up in it. I know that is not a good reason. But it is true. Had I been born a Muslim I expect I should still be one. It may not be a good reason but it is not a discreditable one. In all sorts of ways our beliefs and behaviour are the legacy of our birth and upbringing. To claim that this confers legitimacy on our convictions is nonsense. But to pretend that we can start from a totally clean slate is also nonsense. What is sure is that we should test and examine our inherited beliefs. I hope that had I been born a Muslim I would have rejected parts of the Muslim faith. This entails an examination of the world by human beings which inhabit it. The mere fact that we do this, that we feel the need to examine our beliefs, seems to me to imply that we are other than purely animal. Every time we ask 'Why?' we are behaving in a way which denies determinism. It does not mean that there is a God, but it means that we differ from animals (though we clearly have much in common). My examination of the world makes me think that it depends a great deal on the human mind. I find the objections to Locke's apparently commonsensical view of an external world of substance compelling. I do not say this compels us to belief in an all-pervading mind or prime cause. I am only saying that the world as I know it is so bound up with human perceptions as to be inconceivable without them. Human beings are not some chance product thrown up by evolution, they are prime determinants of their world, though evolution as understood by human beings may be an important factor in it.

So, though I have never had personal experience of God, I have had experiences, indeed all my experience, points to a non-material element in the world. So we come to human beings and their lives. I do not believe that human life is a tale told by an idiot signifying nothing. And I do not believe it because I come up against what to me is the certainty that it is not. It seems to me as certain that there are values as it is that two and two make four. Two and two are only understood to make four by human beings, and that, for instance, the making of money is not the end of existence is also understood by human beings. Here we come up against the peculiarity of the human condition, which is that although I believe it to be as certain that there is a scale of values as it is that two and two make four, yet while the human mind must accept and base its behaviour on the latter, it has some choice both as to what it considers valuable and as to whether it pursues what it believes to be valuable. I find some difficulty over the problem of pain. As for sin, which is the rejection of what is valuable, it seems only explicable if you accept an order of things which is not purely animal. If it is essential to the achievement of virtue that you should choose virtue, though offered the alternative of vice, that does seem to me to suppose that value is more than a purely human concept – if by human you mean something created by the human race. I do not believe that it is true that virtue and a well-run human society are two wholly different matters. On the contrary, I believe that the inefficiency and cruelty of human society are linked to vice. I believe that a society with no values other than success and getting as much material gain as you can would be, and would be seen to be, barbaric. But I also believe that even if we could develop bureaucratic social services to such an extent that all human beings had all choices made for them and that all choices were made rightly it would also be seen to be inhuman because valueless. I do not believe that there is any virtue in enforced virtue and I believe, as I have said, that a belief in virtue is inescapable. The present state of affairs as upheld by the top people seems to me to come near to practising first that material success is everything and secondly that you can run a good society by edict.

So far I would not claim to have come close to a divine or personal God. But there perhaps I do revert to an atavistic belief. And here again it seems to me that this belief is a real part of our existence. I, and I think most people, feel in goodness that there is something divine. I would include in goodness not only moral goodness but masterpieces of art and many and varied activities which have value. And what I would claim to have experienced is the benefit of knowing good people or enjoying their company and benefiting from them. You might call this experiencing the Divine at second-hand. And as I suppose that for those who have had personal experience of God, one of the important results has been the response it evokes, so on occasions when I have been aware of some greatness or goodness, this flows over to me and makes me partake of it just a little. So here morality or pure decision is not enough. So I frequently light a candle when I visit a Catholic church. I do not understand or accept the whole of Roman Catholicism, but the example of some saints seems to me something to be celebrated and it is possible that a little of their virtue may assist me. Like Jonah (one of the most illuminating books in the Bible) to argue with God is part of our divine inheritance but totally to reject the Divine seems contrary to our nature.

26

The Rev. Professor John Polkinghorne

Like all forms of worthwhile activity, science has its share of weary, dull routine, and vexatious frustration. At the end of a working day, the wastepaper-basket of a theoretical physicist is likely to have its fill of crumpled pieces of paper. What then is the reward which keeps men and women at the scientific task? It is, I believe, the desire to understand, and the feeling of wonder which is experienced from time to time at the beautiful structure of the physical world revealed to our collective investigations. The very possibility of theoretical physics results from the deep rational transparency of the universe, the mysterious way in which the patterns of mathematics fit perfectly the patterns of behaviour of the quarks and gluons and electrons, those basic constituents out of which the variety of the world is made. And it is not just any old mathematics which has this power, but rather it is mathematics which in its economy and elegance evokes from its practitioners the epithet 'beautiful'. It has been our experience time and again in the history of physics that the basic equations describing the world have the unmistakable character of mathematical beauty, so that it has become a technique of research to seek theories with this property in the expectation that they will fit the facts. Our prior imaginations, however, are seldom equal to the task, for they need also that experimental nudge of nature which leads physicists to discoveries profoundly satisfying and wonderful in their deep-seated rationality.

I believe that the intellectual joy that scientists feel at the beautiful pattern of the physical world disclosed to them is (whether they acknowledge it or not) an experience of the Divine, for they are privileged to enter into the thoughts of the Creator. The psalmist would agree: 'The heavens are telling the glory of God' (Psalm 19:1). So, in his way, would Einstein:

> The scientist's religious feeling takes the form of a rapturous amazement at the harmony of natural law, which reveals an intelligence of such superiority that, compared with it, all systematic thinking and acting of human beings is an utterly insignificant reflection.

Yet in this manner we encounter only the impersonal side of the divine nature ('The Great Mathematician'). Where are we to meet with a personal God whom we might fittingly call 'Father'?

For me, the answer lies principally in worship. I do not have in mind any extraordinary ecstatic experience, for my own spiritual life has been pretty humdrum. Rather, I refer to the weekly gathering with other Christian people for the celebration of the Eucharist, and the daily routine of saying morning and evening prayer which is my private obligation as an Anglican priest. These provide the sustaining framework of my religious life. The Eucharist is both a remembrance of Jesus's action with his disciples before his sacrificial death upon the cross and also a feast of hope in anticipation of that visible vindication of God's rule which I believe to be our destiny beyond death and history. It is also an experience which is, in a manner I find hard to explain but essential to affirm, a present participation in the life of the Risen Lord. Continually, though not unfailingly, I find sharing in the Eucharist is the occasion for my own deeper spiritual perception of the experience of the Divine. I do not think this is due to the self-induced comfort of a holy huddle, but it is an encounter with Reality. The priestly privilege of celebrating the Eucharist is one I value most highly.

The office (morning and evening prayer) is woven round the psalms (which we say through in the course of every ten weeks) and reading the Bible (a great deal of which is covered in a year). There is a certain routineness (one could also say, faithfulness) involved in doing this, and over the years the words sink into one and become part of one's being. I particularly love the psalms – so much better than any hymn book! There is an honesty and variety of experience recorded there which has proved nourishing to generations of Jews and Christians through the centuries. The psalmists are very bold – they can protest to God, even tell him to wake up (Psalm 44:23), as well as praising him. Their words, and those of scripture generally, are a vehicle for me of encounter with God.

It is also true, I think, that there are prayerful, peaceful places which provide a helpful and natural context for the experience of the Divine. My own spiritual home, in this sense, is a small convent of Anglican nuns located in wooded country in Monmouthshire. I have had an association with this community for a good number of years and I try to visit them each year if I can. People sometimes think that those who follow a relatively enclosed religious life, as these nuns do, are in flight from the world and reality. My experience is quite the reverse. Some of the Sisters are among the most clear-eyed people I know. Spending a few days with them – particularly if one has some time in retreat, a very positive experience of silence broken only by the worship of Chapel – is a real help to me in my spiritual life and development. I do not want to say this sentimentally. I am aware that the peace we find when we visit Tymawr is not costless and that religious communities have their trials and difficulties like any other human body of people. But I do believe that the religious communities of our country, through their prayer and hospitality, play a largely hidden but essential role in fostering the experience of the Divine.

27

The Very Rev. Christopher Lewis

God is always and everywhere; that is what they say! Yet we experience the Divine, if at all, in certain special places or on particular occasions. Now and again I believe I sense the presence of God in well-known holy places like the crypt of Canterbury Cathedral or indeed at religious services. For me, however, it is often when taking strenuous exercise in striking surroundings that I think I experience the Divine.

I ran in the London Marathon; that was a high-point and the one on which I would like to reflect. I expect that pride comes into it, for I am proud that I finished. Yet the key experience was that of padding along with others for mile after mile, united by a common purpose and encouraged by thousands of people who were supporting everyone indiscriminately. There were flags and bunting, hi-fi sets in the windows with the speakers turned towards the world (in contrast to the individualism of the walkman) and everywhere colour, laughter and sweat: a wonderfully tasteless foretaste of heaven. In me there was the sense that this is how things are meant to be: the unity of people, the rhythm of life, the body and the spirit working in unison. Also, I felt the importance not only of journeying (inner journeys never seem to arrive anywhere!) but of getting there: the wonder of arriving and knowing that a welcome awaits. I got there and received the little gifts which everyone gets. My position at 16,222nd was not distinguished, and ten minutes for each mile is consistent but not quick. Most of our efforts are quite pedestrian.

The experience had a number of sides to it. First there was carnival. Nobody can feel that there is no hope for humanity when people are taking to the streets in such numbers for purposes which seem wholly admirable. I expect that there were sinister forces at work here, as there are in any situation, perhaps in the minds of the makers of running shoes or in the desperation of one or two to win. Yet on Marathon Day the sentiments which triumph among spectators and participants alike are co-operative and loving. Sometimes humankind does not appear in the best light and the image of God is hard to discern, but on Marathon Day there is no difficulty.

Humour is crucial. Sometimes people write books on the therapeutic value of humour or on its sociology, thereby rendering it serious. It is better to share in the experience of people sending themselves and others up with happy abandon. That is quite simply a sign of transcendence: a sign that there is far more to life than the realists will admit. Many ways of making that point can be found, but one is to run twenty-six miles in a gorilla suit having water-fights with children along the way.

The exertion was a necessary part. Physical effort is fundamental to life, perhaps ever since we had to run after or away from animals and enemies. As people have become more holistic in their thinking, so the place of exercise in the balanced life has been stressed. For myself, I feel unable to pray or to live life to the full without some kind of daily routine which stretches the body as well as the soul. Before I pray each morning I do exercises and the two go together. Sometimes I do both at once, with the rhythm of the one feeding the rhythm of the other. In the Marathon, the encouragement to greater physical effort gives the event a common appeal which can be immediately communicated to all ages and types of people; it is a universal experience. When the pain becomes acute, you bear some of it yourself but also turn to others, knowing that they know how you feel.

Ironically, the charity for which I was raising sponsorship money was the Leprosy Mission and they had a number of supporters who wrote in and objected to the fact that the Marathon was run on a Sunday and that they were thus associated with an event which interrupted Sunday observance. I pointed out that I found the rhythm of running, and the pure joy of the occasion, conducive to prayer and worship, but I think that I was not understood.

Needless to say, the Marathon has an admirable balance between the individual and the collective, something frequently lost when people talk of their religious experiences. It is the individual who pounds along and yet the accompanying music is that of cheers and of the gentle flapping of hundreds of flat feet. In among the countless individuals are teams and groupings, friendships and conversations. There is nothing to fear. The rescue teams are there and you can always walk, in the comfort of knowing that others will be walking too.

Lastly, running takes place out of doors. The great outdoors is common property, common ground. It is a meeting place where I can be met by God and by other people without the particular expectations of special buildings.

That is enough of one experience. When I reflect on it, I find it hard to believe that it is not of God. Certainly, it was an experience of the Divine for me: the Divine in a secular event. Experiences of God for me are to do with life in general, yet summed up and focused in the particular. Of course, the Marathon is open to all sorts of questions. Is it masochistic? Is the euphoric sense merely that which is experienced in any crowd? Is not the camaraderie fleeting? Is it all just male pride in brute strength? If it is indicative of God, is it not the fierce muscular God of the Victorian public school?

Perhaps some of these questions do undermine my experience. Yet I would ask why the aesthetes should have all the 'spirituality'. Why can the hearties not have some of it and why can they not wrest it out into the market place? For the spiritual always seems to be associated with retreat, inactivity, individualism, quiet and a lack of political action. Of course people justify such emphases as a preparation for action, but somehow the action seldom comes. Books about the spiritual have covers spread with daffodils or with pictures of mysteriously winding paths devoid of humanity. They are all very foreign to my experience of the Divine, which is collective and active and involved with the poor. The spiritual writer Evelyn Underhill was finally persuaded to concern herself with the poor, but then gave the game away by observing that it was justified because it did her soul good. Tolstoy is said to have said: 'Peace and quiet are nothing but meanness of the soul.' I do not agree with that statement and suspect that Tolstoy did not either; yet the saying points to a danger as great as any stemming from frenetic activity.

The Benedictines had it right at least in theory. Yet in practice what often went wrong in their great balance of prayer study and work was that the work slipped, the physical aspect of life was neglected as it was taken on by lay brothers. So they became spiritual in a narrow sense, or at times they just became decadent and had to be reminded of the value of the physical, for example by the Cistercians.

Much modern spirituality (the very term is incipiently Manichaean) represents a distancing from the physical and material, a retreat into pietism. The Christian may quite legitimately, like Jesus in the garden of Gethsemane, be at times mainly concerned with retreat and reflection. But on the whole he or she should be out and about in God's world, doing his business. So when people talk of their 'journeys' I think of the Marathon!

28

The Rev. Professor Leslie Houlden

The date is 1948, the place northern Germany. A young soldier, doing his national service between school and university, goes gladly to spend a weekend at one of the Army Chaplains' Department's retreat and conference houses. In the strange, far-off conditions of an army of occupation, it is housed in a lovely close at Preetz, once a convent but turned at the Reformation into a home for elderly gentlewomen (and did the personnel really change?). The church was medieval, with some baroque embellishments and an organ from the time of J.S. Bach.

The soldier was a smart grammar-school boy, on the fashionable edge between agnosticism and atheism, with momentary pangs of faith, persisting from a once-loved immersion in the Church's worship. To it he remained attached by the strong, thin thread of organ-playing. A muddle of music, wistfulness, friends and barrack boredom had brought him to Preetz.

Perhaps it was late August, Augustine's day. The chaplain preached on the saint's laborious, tortuous movement to faith: with his Christian home, his so clever intellectualism, his embracing of first this philosophy then that, his emotional trials – and then the garden and the voice from over the wall, *Tolle, lege*, 'Take and read': the reading and faith. From then, no going back; yet certainly no static faith, but much movement and profound heart-searching on issue after issue, some of them affecting lives as well as minds.

The sermon was the soldier's *Tolle, lege*, with its invitation (as it seemed) to presumptuous identification with that other grammar-school boy, of fourth-century North Africa. No doubt my memory (I step forward!) of that day is inaccurate and friends would say how former thoughts still filled my speech (just as Augustine still wrote like a Platonist well into his supposed Christian years). All the same, it was the day of no return.

How important memory is in Christian experience. Augustine saw it as the point of our deepest affinity with God. We feed on what has been given to *us*. I count myself fortunate that I was nourished (with the preacher as mediator) by one who was manifestly indebted for ever to the ideas he had held before his day of no return. With elements of acceptance, alteration and rejection, they continued to 'make' him. So I have never felt tempted to decline manifest truth, from whatever quarter, in the name of a sealed, intra-mural Christian truth, embattled against too-readily defined falsehood.

In that way, the day of no return was not an end but a new beginning with the prospect of constant development, but now on a new footing. A beginning, but also a return to roots deeper still. For memory reaches deeper than adolescent self-important arrogance to childhood gifts of home and plodding church. Nothing is lost or in vain.

A benefit of this style of debt to memory is that it precludes contentment with its present vantage point. My recollection of Preetz is surely imperfect. My memory of the whole past is formed by my present, and certainly I hope to see it differently in the future. In other terms, relationship with God can no more be content with a valued past than any other relationship that hopes to flourish.

It is partly that beginnings, if powerful, are woefully narrow. I was so concerned about whether there was God or not and whether little (big!) *I* could believe in him that I had no idea what such believing might entail or demand. No idea, for example, of its implications for the structures of our society, or of where my gaps in awareness lay. Training for the ministry in the fifties was hotter on the devout life of the individual than on either the theological or the social dimension. I served a curacy in the most deprived part of a northern city without ever seeing our work in other than ecclesiastical terms – strengthening the faithful and increasing their number, helping particular people on their personal journeys. It was a very limited perception of the gospel.

And the theological attitudes referred to above, especially the openness in principle to movement and discovery, were slow to have effect in numerous areas of belief. Only slowly did I come to see that if I thought X, then surely I ought to be thinking Y. Yet at each stage I have tended to feel what a coherent whole my outlook makes! And that, of course, has always been a regrettable piece of complacency – an instinctive comfort that was quite contrary to the spirit of my day of no return.

About 1950, I attended, in Oxford, an enactment of the Eucharist as it might have been in Hippo in Augustine's day. (The evidence is fragmentary and the reconstruction had to be made from references in his own writings.) Memory, movement – and continuity. The outward face of the Eucharist (words, atmosphere, 'staging') has altered more, in Western Catholic Christendom, in the past thirty years than for centuries, and many feel the *dis*continuity keenly. I have always felt the reverse aspect of the matter. Here is an experience of the Christian mystery (faith, prayer, attitudes, agonies all concentrated and encapsulated) which unites me through time with Augustine, and of course back through him to the beginning in Jesus. There is a way of seeing that point which is pure romanticism. But in another (and healthier?) mood, it is another instance of memory as a key element in our experience of God. Christians are not alone in making much of it, if only to establish reliable marks of identity: Christianity after all comes in almost every conceivable size and shape. We all need such marks of identity if we are not to be dazzled in the religious supermarket. But the marks should be few, lest we tie God down to some past situation and ourselves to some phase we should outgrow. Oddly, however, it is the age-long marks, like the Eucharist, which may also speak loudest for modernity – for experience of God now. Here, for me at least, is the repeated happening which most perfectly embraces the many facets of the Christian jewel and of life in its bitter-sweet reality.

In one way, I do not approve of an article like this! Experience of God is so bound up with personal history that much of it can mean little to others, and may merely pander to inquisitiveness. Worse still, it brings out one's tendency to put the best possible construction upon oneself. Readers may be daunted by the seeming paragons whose lives they briefly enter. On the other hand, as Augustine and Preetz showed me decisive truth one Sunday many years ago, so other identifications may in their turn succeed. In this sphere, masters and apprentices arise at random.

There are, of course, no guarantees that one is not deluded. But that sense of uncertainty is part of the price of openness. It is the dark side of readiness for days of no return which are not ends but beginnings.

29

The Rev. Canon Christopher Hill

In more than one community of faith there has been a recent upsurge of fundamentalism. One characteristic of this is a certainty of divine experience, of what God is saying to the human race, or to his people. This is coupled with a literalistic interpretation of the sacred scriptures of that faith.

Conversely, there is a fascinating strand of religious agnosticism to be found in the teachings and writings of many religious mystics; people who claim an authentic experience of the divine but who express this experience reticently and negatively.

Within the Christian tradition this 'way of unknowing' was first charted in an extensive way by the author of a corpus of mystical writings whom we now call (because of earlier misidentification) Dionysius the Pseudo-Areopagite, who flourished in about 500, probably in Syria. 'Dionysius' had a profound and extensive influence on Christian thought in both East and West. Much of his teaching derives from Neoplatonism and represents a fascinating synthesis between Christianity and the mysticism of the late classical world. Moreover, similar teachings can be found in both Jewish and Islamic syntheses with Neoplatonism.

In England during the Middle Ages the influence of the 'way of unknowing' was large, especially during the fourteenth century when mysticism flowered in this country as it had never done before and has never done since. The author of *The Cloud of Unknowing* shows the influence of Pseudo-Dionysius on every page. So also does Julian of Norwich; she speaks explicitly (if historically incorrectly) of 'Saint Dionyse of France'.

Evelyn Underhill indeed saw a permanent distinction between two types of mysticism; the way of affirmation and the way of negation. Two different ways in which men and women claim to experience the Divine:

> In its description, all mystics will be found to lean to one side or the other, to the affirmative or negative element which it contains. The austere mysticism of Eckhart and his followers, their temperamental sympathy with the Neoplatonic language of Dionysius the Areopagite,

> caused them to describe it – and also very often the higher state of contemplation to which it leads – as above all things an emptiness, a divine dark, an ecstatic deprivation. They will not profane its deep satisfactions by the inadequate terms proper to earthly peace and joy: and, true to their school, fall back on the paradoxically suggestive powers of negation.

All this is by way of preface to something more autobiographical. As a Christian I make no claim to having ever experienced a 'conversion' in the sense of a decisive once-for-all emotional experience which has instantly changed my life. Some Christians would therefore deny that I am a Christian. Nor can I claim that I have ever experienced anything which I would dare to call direct revelation. I am suspicious of all such claims.

I also find there are other Christians like me in other Churches and other believers like me in other communities of faith.

This is not to say that I believe that human beings cannot have a true experience of God. But that I believe that such experience is never in this life immediate. Though some religious teachers in all faiths use the analogies of human joy, warmth, love (like St Teresa of Avila or John Wesley); they *remain* analogies. For me, at least, the way of unknowing seems safer by its recognition that, though God may be experienced in joy, warmth and love, he remains beyond these human experiences.

I can remember my first reading of the poetry of T.S. Eliot. And of using this passage in meditation:

> I said to my soul, be still, and wait without hope
> For hope would be hope for the wrong thing; wait without love
> For love would be love of the wrong thing; there is yet faith
> But the faith and the love and the hope are all in the waiting.
> Wait without thought, for you are not ready for thought:
> So the darkness shall be the light, and the stillness the dancing.
> ...
> To arrive where you are, to get from where you are not,
> You must go by a way wherein there is no ecstasy.
> In order to arrive at what you do not know
> You must go by a way which is the way of ignorance.
> In order to possess what you do not possess
> You must go by the way of dispossession.
> In order to arrive at what you are not

You must go through the way in which you are not.
And what you do not know is the only thing you know
And what you own is what you do not own
And where you are is where you are not.

East Coker III

And from there I traced my way back through other writings of the way of unknowing: for me this has been an authentic experience of the Divine and yet one which, because of its agnosticism, can also be shared by others of different traditions.

There is, however, another area of some importance to me personally in my religious pilgrimage which at first sight might seem to sit uneasily with this negative approach to experiencing the Divine: the sacraments. I can think of times, especially in the first bewilderment of experiencing critical Biblical scholarship as a theological student, when I was not sure I believed in God or in the divinity of Jesus Christ, but I was, paradoxically, quite certain about the 'Real Presence' of Christ in the Christian Eucharist. It is an interesting feature of Catholic modernism that sacramental faith and practice can remain firm in spite of agnosticism.

On reflection I do not think the 'via negativa' and a strong sacramentalism are in logical conflict. Significantly, Dionysius devotes a considerable amount of his writings to the Christian sacraments. Moreover, rightly understood the sacraments are 'mysteries' – the word used by Eastern Orthodox Christians. The Western word sacrament means 'sign': something which points beyond itself. So sacraments, like the human signs of communication we use every day such as the smile, the embrace, the communal meal, mediate realities deeper than the conceptual or the verbal. But these realities are never experienced immediately, always through, with and under sanctified human actions and words. Christian theologians, Catholic, Protestant and Orthodox have rightly insisted that it is through faith that the inward meaning of the sacraments is made clear. Though sacraments are visible, tangible and audible, their significance requires the insight of faith to see beyond and through the outward sign to the inner mystery. However real the experience of God is through the sacramental it is never direct and unmediated, it never bypasses the created and human order. So the sacraments, too, are an indirect experience of the Divine and not incompatible with the 'via negativa' of the mystic.

Put the negative mystical tradition together with the sacramental and you have a considerable body of historic religious experience. I find this comforting as I contemplate the strident fundamentalisms of the contemporary religious scene with their absolute certainties about the direct communication of God to humankind. I believe God does reveal himself to us; but in this life never as he is in himself. The recognition of this will make us reticent and humble in the claims religious men and women make about God. But also closer to the truth which the religious believer holds that he or she will one day see face to face rather than as now through a glass, darkly.

30

The Rev. Dr John Vincent

In my view, 'experiencing the Divine' takes place when people put themselves into a discipleship relation to some great religious leader or movement or system or philosophy.

In this sense, I see discipleship as working within a number of different religious and non-religious systems. Within the spectrum of the wide experience of humanity as a whole, individuals may choose their own discipleship. That is, they can choose whichever Master or Mistress or System or Philosophy they will follow.

All religious systems have their origin in some outstanding figure, be it Prophet, Guru, Avatar or Divine Figure. Each figure had disciples in their own lifetime; each today has disciples. Each figure makes a Way for the disciples to follow. Each figure provides a model, and teachings, and dramatic exemplary stories which become formative for the disciples and in the light of which the disciples create their own ways.

This is extremely relevant in our time. Dialogue between devotees of varied religious convictions and practices often leads to no communication at all. But conversation between disciples of different ways often reveals that certain practices bring us alongside each other. The classic Five Pillars of Moslem faith are Creed, Prayer, Almsgiving, Fasting and Pilgrimage. Such elements occur in various forms in most religions, and certainly in Christianity. In these areas, the patterns of basic religion are very comparable. However, the *distinctiveness* of any one religion lies elsewhere, precisely because the simple externals of most faiths look so similar.

In the present century, the determining influence of the lives of Karl Marx among Communists and of Lenin among Soviet Communists shows that the discipleship phenomenon and relationship can exist outside the religious sphere and yet achieve there comparable results. The faith of humanism does the same, often based upon the lifestyle of classic humanist figures.

Discipleship is thus the *reality* indicated in and facilitated by 'religions' and by systems like religions. They bear witness to the persistence of the notion that, on the level of common humanity, there are individuals who seem to have 'intimations of immortality', and who thus attract disciples.

This, in my view, is the beginning and end of it.

I do not think I know anything about 'experiencing the Divine', if by this is meant some kind of experience of phenomena outside my normal life, or some experience of the numinous, Otto's *mysterium tremendum et fascinans*. Whether such a 'divine realm' exists, I do not know. I only know that I have not experienced it. Nor can I claim that God has ever spoken to me, or called me by name, or revealed anything to me that I could not account for without that hypothesis.

This does not mean that with Voltaire 'I have no need of that hypothesis' – notably God or the Divine. Neither would I care to exclude the possibility of it, or deny its existence to those who claim to have experienced it. But I personally draw a blank on it all.

My faith has not come that way.

There, now, I have used another slippery word, 'faith'. There is a great debate about that too, and I have to dissent there also from some commonly adopted positions.

'Faith', according to Hebrews 11:1, is 'the substance of things hoped for, the evidence of things not seen'. Or it is what Luther called 'a sure trust' in the mercies of God? Or it is what Wesley called the personal knowledge of a right relationship with God? Beyond that, in common parlance, faith is the ability to believe in unproven or invisible things, such as the existence of God, or of heaven, or of God's providence.

Again, I draw a blank. I have no such faith as any of these.

But I think I have faith such as is referred to by the New Testament, and particularly the Gospels.

In the Gospels, 'faith' is the human ability to persuade oneself that a miracle can happen to me, or that I may myself become part of a miracle. Jesus says to people, 'If you have faith, I can heal you.' The special powers of the Master are released by a calling forth from within the would-be healed person. Or Jesus says to would-be disciples, 'If you leave all, you can become a disciple.' Faith consists in abandonment to the new Way. Or Jesus says, 'If you had faith, you could move mountains.' Discipleship consists in confronting and dismantling oppressing powers.

This kind of discipleship-faith is as far as I get towards 'experiencing the Divine'. It is very materialistic, practical, mundane, secular. The theological justification for that is the Christian doctrine of Incarnation. God is not known in the mystery of his essence, is not experienced in his total otherness. Rather, God is known as a human being, and experienced as a style of being human in the midst of humanity. God is to be encountered in the man Jesus. Those who would encounter God do so by 'playing the same game', acting the same way, imitating the same attitudes, as were displayed in Jesus.

Three implications follow from this.

First of all, that Christianity as discipleship is basically about personal lifestyle and practical commitment. It is not first about ideas, or values, or spirituality, or systems. It is first and foremost about what I do with my life, where I put my body.

I have often put it this way: Jesus never asked people to believe in him with their head. He did not even ask people to love him with their heart. He asked people to follow him with their feet. Once the feet are going in a certain direction, the head and heart follow. And the heart learns to love where the whole body is; and the head learns to justify where the whole body is.

So, we today have to be 'out there', with actual disciples, models, projects and opportunities that others can become discipled to. The evidence is that people become disciples when there are people and projects present in the world for possible disciples to become associated with.

This, of course, means that if we are going to have people and locations where this is to be encountered, they need to be rather more radical forms of Christianity that most churches represent. But that is good news for those who seek new forms of the Church, as many do today, or who see the importance of outstanding individuals at all levels of society who embody and live out radical discipleship.

This certainly was true in my own life. Early in my teens, I became fascinated by the figure of Jesus, and felt drawn to him. But it was the actual embodiment of aspects of Jesus's character in other people which provided the environment and the model for such fascination. A gentle schoolmaster, not many years older than myself – Tony Stocks – opened his home to a few of us. Teachers in a theological college – J.T. Wilkinson and Percy Scott – invited me in. Figures I sought out and learned from – Donald Soper and George MacLeod – provided models and stimuli.

The discipleship-faith which I see as 'experiencing the Divine' was thus discipleship-faith and apprenticeship to and learning from other disciples. There is thus in discipleship a chain of discipleship-relationship which goes from generation to generation, and ultimately back to Jesus Christ himself.

All we need is living disciples today who can be surrogate-Masters, or better, co-apprentices.

Secondly, this discipleship-faith needs to be visible in some project or programme. Discipleship-faith is commitment with others in being part of a *movement*, actions in history, which are larger than the disciple group itself.

It seems quite clear to me that the purpose of Jesus was to inaugurate a radically new set of human relationships which would subvert the existing orders of Jewish and Roman society. By his standing alongside the disadvantaged, by his proclamation of blessedness in the poor, by his calling as disciples those outside and hostile to the normal hierarchies, Jesus was attempting to set up an alternative society within the societies of his own day.

To this 'project' he gave the name, 'God's blessing', or 'God's happening', or 'God's Realm'. Our term, 'the Kingdom of God' utilises top-downwards, hierarchical terms. But what Jesus was announcing and creating was a radically alternative, bottom-upwards, society of mutuality, love, modesty and sustainability. This he intended for everyone. The disciple-group was the experimental out-station, the microcosm, of what was intended to be everywhere and for everyone. It was to be a place and state where God's will could be done on earth.

This Project of Jesus has achieved contemporary actuality at various times in history, in varying ways. But it remains as a lasting call to be pioneering for the sake of new humanities, in every age and time. Discipleship-faith is political, economic and social both in its radical import within the disciple groups, and also in its witness to the whole of society in which the reigning powers of greed, affluence, racism, sexism and classism must be constantly opposed. And all this not merely because they are evil in themselves, but because they are irreconcilable to the Project of a Divine Realm on earth. In the contemporary scene, a British Liberation Theology best expresses all this.

Thirdly, the discipleship-faith has to produce experimental outstations, visible embodiments in new communities.

Looking back on my life, a great deal of it has been spent in this area. The Divine Realm, it seemed to me, became credible at least in part because of human communities, especially intentional communities. I learned from J.T. Wilkinson about the early Methodists, I joined Donald Soper's Order of Christian Witness, I spent time in George MacLeod's Iona Community.

From them I learned that community was not some ideal, but rather the necessary bread-and-butter of divinity on earth, the necessary grime and glory of the incarnate deity. Paul in I Corinthians 12:12 talks of Christians together as 'the Body of Christ', in which there are different members performing different vital functions.

So, much of my life has been spent in helping to create mini-communities within which particular vocations, 'charisms' and missions might be held together and fostered. The Ashram Community (1967), the Urban Theology Unit (1969) and the Sheffield Inner City Ecumenical Mission (1971) are still the communities within which I work, whose disparate and special styles and people are parts of the way in which the Divine agenda is made possible for me.

Thus, the Divine makes its claims upon me – or perhaps even I facilitate the Divine in practice.

To discover more, I feel increasingly the need to dig deeper, rather than to expand more widely. The priorities I have named – personal discipleship, discipleship to a movement for social change, and discipleship as embodiment in alternative community – are all ways that demand more time and depth and commitment than I have managed yet. But there is always tomorrow.

31

The Very Rev. Alan Webster

Traditional Christian teaching about the experience of God is concerned with God as transcendent and God as immanent. My experience has been more of God as immanent than of God as transcendent, though I believe in both aspects of the presence of God. To use an analogy beloved of the greatest mystical teacher of this century, Baron von Huegel, God is both about the cornfields, sugar beet and marshes of Norfolk, and about the astonishing Alpen Rose and Edelweiss of the Mountains. God is both more humanly intimate and more mysteriously over against than much Christian teaching succeeds in conveying. The Divine is in the work and decencies of society and family as well as in the Direct Vision of God found in prayer and worship. God is reflected in all nature as well as in super-nature, in the dim background and commonsense of our living and the careful discoveries of science, as well as in the moments when we sense 'the Beautitude of Heaven ... the love of our enemies ... and eager acceptance of suffering' (Baron von Huegel).

From early years I have found both faith and doubt, fear and acceptance, in experiencing nature and the night sky. Friendship and the struggles for justice, unhurried conversation as well as slow growth in the love and care of others can be places of revelation. Historical religion, incarnate in a Lakeland jewel such as Cartmell, Fell Chapel or Norwich Cathedral or St Paul's, especially at some moment of worship, emphasises the transcendent. Looking back, my experience of God comes through different elements, historical, intellectual and mystical. In this brief essay I concentrate on the insights of a particular woman in a particular place as they affected a celebration of worship in the 1970s, which reveal both transcendent and immanent experiences of the Divine.

To come as a stranger to Norwich and to share in its political, social and religious life made me aware in 1970 of the extreme need to listen and learn and admire a special community in one's own country. Ronald Blythe's *Akenfield* and his Divine Landscapes introduced the story of country people surviving harsh conditions and still producing radical heroes, the rebel leader Kett in the sixteenth century and those who supported the Burston school strike as an assertion of village and

Christian socialist rights in the twentieth. The unspoken Norfolk motto 'Du different', exemplified in Edith Cavell, made me hope to experience once again those words of the Psalms, 'All my fresh springs shall be in thee.'

May 8, 1373, is the only date mentioned in Julian of Norwich's tiny mystical treatise *Revelations of Divine Love*. I wondered whether the Cathedral and city, the shrine of Julian and the county, ought to be invited to remember the 600th anniversary. I put this question on the agenda of the Bishop's staff meeting – caution was advised. Was Julian really sound or too obscure or too well locked away from normal life, her mind overfull of anxieties, possibly pathological nightmares such as the apparition of the face of Christ bleeding from the cross? Was she healthy? She was walled up by a bishop. Why not concentrate on Bunyan's *Pilgrim's Progress*, or Edith Cavell's martyrdom or some contemporary adventure such as the founding of the University of East Anglia? Admittedly Julian was the first woman to write a book in English and T.S. Eliot had quoted her in his *Four Quartets*, but was there a link between this remote English mystic and our contemporary search for spirituality – after all the changes of the 1960s?

I tried living with some of Julian's aphorisms to see whether the Spirit still spoke the same language 'No one can separate himself from anyone else ...'. By chance a TV guru, Canon Peter Freeman, arranged a programme 'The Big Question', which for ten years appeared weekly on Wednesdays at midnight. He invited Father Eric Boyle of the Catholic Order of Friars Minor, who shared St Francis's wit and longing for the Gospel to be heard and freshly interpreted, Edmund Banyard, an East Anglian leading Free Churchman, very knowledgeable about scientific research, and myself to answer questions on an extempore television programme always using the language of the outside world. We were on the margin of Christian language – frequently criticised or appreciated for not using the insider language of the churches.

I went on reading Julian while preparing for these programmes, remembering that she wrote in English and not in Latin or French, longing to bridge the cultural gap between the ruling groups in society and with a plea for love and care, suffering and discipleship. The fact that Julian used the analogies of normal life, the nut in the palm of your hand, the washing blown by the wind (no doubt at the city laundry not far from her cell), and her dream of walking, perhaps on the North Norfolk coast, at the bottom of the sea, feeling the all-surrounding support of the Divine, suggested to me that this is how the spirit may be appreciated. When we went together to talk with prisoners in Norwich Prison, or took the programme to the incurables in hospital, or the gravely incapacitated in Stoke Mandeville, it felt as though the incapacitated, the incurables and the prisoners began to speak the divine words of encouragement, 'All shall be well and all shall be well and all manner of thing shall be well.'

Meditation on Julian led me to grasp that experience of the Divine is often linked to counselling. Many came to Julian in her cell, though only her conversation with Margery Kemp of Lynn is recorded. Her insistence that knowledge of God is found in personal loving relationships, in grace as it links humans to each other and to Jesus Christ, led to the conviction that the expulsion of the Divine in so many of the horrors of our century, both wars and the Final Solution, came from a devilish determination to keep oneself separate from other races, other churches, other routes to God. Slowly it dawned that the Divine Spirit required the Close to become the Open and the growing counselling centres, the Samaritans, the Citizens Advice Bureau, the centres for healing as well as the statutory services both medical and social were avenues trod by the Divine. The Student Counselling Centre at the University became for me as much a place of the Spirit as the University Chaplaincy. Brian Thorne in his 'Person-centred Counselling Therapeutic and Spiritual Dimensions' published in 1991 has given a theological justification for this conviction. Here are chapters on the God who comes on Good Friday, the quality of tenderness and the place of intimacy, which fuse the insights of Christianity and those of professional counselling.

Serving the whole community in Julian's city led me to share her experience that the Divine Spirit loves humanity, even when the Spirit is explicitly rejected. Julian had taught that there is no anger in God, no rejection. One year the Lord Mayor of Norwich was a former member of the Communist Party and an explicit agnostic. Anxious that the traditional Lord Mayor's service in the Cathedral should not compel him to do violence to his convictions, I asked whether he would prefer not to read a lesson lest he felt forced by social convention to violate his principles. 'No,' he replied. 'Find a lesson from the Old Testament which condemns the rich who do not concern themselves with mercy and justice.' Shortly afterwards he came to ask whether the Dean and Chapter would provide accommodation in the Close for Ugandan Asians, homeless thanks to the tyranny of General Amin.

We found a house. Soon after, we co-operated in the founding of a Third World centre and the Norwich Night Shelter, now the St Martin's Housing Trust, which fifteen years later accommodates between 100 and 200 homeless men and women. In all this I experienced God and realised that God's Spirit could use those who do not explicitly call upon the Divine. Reflecting, meditating, praying, worrying about these difficult concerns, whose success often involved risks and complex negotiations, gave me the sense that God is at work and can be felt in the life and tasks of the modern city.

So many modern religious institutions insist on exclusiveness; saying the Creed, having a particular attitude to the Bible, a rule of church attendance. All these religious habits may be joyful, but they may also become ways of criticising those who ask questions or looking down on those who have an alternative lifestyle or do not go to church. As I read and re-read Julian and considered the fact that she was on the margins of the institutional church, I consulted others whom I knew valued her, themselves living wholly in the world. Alec Guinness told me that he used to 'scurry to Julian of Norwich' when he felt oppressed. He was astonished and delighted by her assurance that the hazelnut round as a ball, the symbol of all that is made, so dangerously fragile and small, lasts and ever shall last for 'God loveth it, God made it, God keepeth it'. Years later he was given a hazelnut made of rare gold to be worn as a buttonhole and to go with him as a reminder of the truth about God and the Universe.

In Julian's words:

> You would learn our Lord's meaning in this vision?
> Learn it well. Love was his meaning.
> Who showed it you? Love.
> Hold on to this and you will learn
> And understand Love more and more.
> But you will not know or learn
> Anything else – ever.

My experience of the Divine Presence was as much in the secular and in the immanent as my experience Sunday after Sunday, day after day in the worship of the Cathedral.

But I did experience the Divine in the Cathedral at a great celebration of Julian in May 1973. Hundreds came from Norfolk and Norwich as well as from London and New York, France and Rome. It was an Ecumenical Eucharist with the Superior General of the Order of Notre Dame herself coming from Rome to read a passage from Julian. The preacher was a Jesuit. The Chairman of the Methodist District concelebrated the Eucharist in the Nave with me and other Anglican clergy, and the final blessing was given by the Anglican Bishop, the Roman Catholic Bishop and other Free Church leaders. The communicants, Catholic, Anglican and Protestant, were showered from the clerestory of the Cathedral during the final hymn with rose petals slowly descending in the clear East Anglian sunlight, and left on procession through the city to the Shrine, clutching hazelnuts. I felt a strange movement of the spirit as Christians rose above the barriers which had barred them from sharing Communion or accepting the leadership of women. Nuns from France joined their Anglican sisters and gathered up the rose petals into their missals. The churches have not yet found a way to include women amongst their leaders, but on this occasion Sister Maria Reynolds, Monica Furlong, Etta Gullick and Dr Lorna Kendall all joined in the Julian Consultation and led us far on our way in the understanding and the experience of Divine Love. Perhaps because Julian had insisted that we should consider the motherhood of God and even Christ as our mother as well as our brother, I experienced at the Cathedral the divine joy, as I had never experienced it before.

In kindling our imagination, God can lead us back from religion as private and individualistic, to reclaim the high ground of relationships and politics and economics and the way cities actually work. Politics and mysticism, prayer and the conception of planet Earth resting in the hand of God are all fused together and it is at this moment of dynamism and poetry and vision that worship takes hold of us and leads us to experience God utterly other and yet close to our heart. This was what Julian gave me in her city in the 1970s.

32

Mrs Mary Whitehouse

It is only now, looking back over a period of eighty-one years, that I can see how the Lord's hand was in so many situations that looked bad at the time! Take, for example, my bout of malignant tertian malaria which, the specialist told us, kills three out of four people unless treated at once.

We had been on holiday in the Gambia in the late 1950s and it was only after we had been home for several months that my bouts of total exhaustion and periodic acute shivering were finally diagnosed. Mercifully, that particular type of malaria does not recur, but I was left without the usual energy and vitality which had enabled me to cope with a large three-storey Victorian house and three strapping sons.

We could not afford domestic help but we decided that if I could get a part-time teaching job then we could. I went to see the education officer in Wolverhampton, and sought his help. 'I would only want to teach art' – my subject – 'and I would want to be able to get my children off to school before I left my house and be back before they were,' I said. 'Dear me,' he replied rather reprovingly, 'I'm afraid it's highly unlikely that we shall be able to find anything to suit you.'

But within a week he had done just that – teaching art part-time in a school just around the corner. Within two years we moved house, the boys were leaving school and I was appointed Senior Mistress – 'responsible for the welfare of the girls' and head of the Art Department in a large secondary modern school in what is now Telford New Town.

In my capacity as Senior Mistress I was immediately involved in some pioneering work in the field of sex education which, according to the newly published Newsom Report, should be given on a basis of 'chastity before marriage and fidelity within it' – which is how I would have wished to do it anyway.

This was at the beginning of the 1960s, at the time of the launching of the so-called 'New Morality' and the take-over of the BBC in particular by its advocates. It was out of my experience of the impact of television upon the children for whom I was then responsible that the work in which I have been involved for the last twenty-eight years has grown – and all, I think to myself sometimes, because I contracted malaria!

And looking back, one can see how if one gives one's life to God, as I did in my early twenties, He does indeed take us at our word even though He does not necessarily make His purposes clear at the time.

Another turning-point came after our announcement – the 'our' represents the Rev. and Mrs Basil Buckland, my husband Ernest and myself! – of the launching of the 'Clean Up TV Campaign' in January 1964. Totally inexperienced and callow as far as the press was concerned, I found myself being led into very deep water by the first journalist who came to see me – 'Will you be holding a public meeting, Mrs Whitehouse?' Hadn't thought of it actually, but I took a deep breath and said, 'Yes, we will.' 'Where will you hold it – Birmingham Town Hall?' – asked the man from the *Birmingham Evening Mail*. Another deep breath and I said, 'Yes.' So there we were, just the four of us committed to filling a hall that held 2,000 seats!

The day of the meeting I kept praying, 'Lord – please give us 250', thinking that if that number of people arrived then the press couldn't say the hall was empty! In the event – described in the next day's *Times* 'as one of the most remarkable meetings ever held in the Birmingham Town Hall' – thirty-seven coach-loads arrived from all over the country, from places as far apart as Devon and Scotland, and the hall was full to overflowing! But the opposition was there too. Several long-haired 'trendies' jumped onto the platform and tried to grab my microphone, but I was quickly rescued, while a couple of rows of nuns stamped their feet and led everyone in the singing of 'Jerusalem'. Suddenly I found myself saying, 'Ladies, Gentlemen – far from being the culmination of our campaign, this is but the beginning!' And so it was. The National Viewers' and Listeners' Association was born and the years since have been full of experiences of the way the Lord has gone before.

And not, of course, only in the big events. Over the years, especially when they are filled with situations for which one has no previous experience, one comes to depend more and more on the belief that God has it all in His hands and that He will honour what we do in His service.

33

The Rev. Canon Peter Pilkington

In *Summoned by Bells* John Betjeman writes:

> Some know for all their lives that Christ is God,
> Some start upon that arduous love affair
> In clouds of doubt and argument; and some
> (My closest friends) seem not to want His love –
> And why this is I wish to God I knew.
> ... The steps to truth were made by sculptured stone
> Stained glass and vestments, holy-water stoups
> Incense and crossings of myself – the things
> That hearty middle-stumpers most despise,
> As 'all the inessentials of the Faith'.

In some ways this mirrors my experience. My remote ancestors left Suffolk in the early nineteenth century to find a better life in the developing industrial north. Durham in the nineteenth century drew immigrants from all over the British Isles, escaping from rural poverty to share in the opportunities created by the growth of the coalfields and factories. One great-grandfather was a clock-maker, another a miner (from Somerset), illiterate but an ardent non-conformist. Most of my family professed a nominal Anglicanism, but so far as I know none of them took part in any active religious life. Like many nineteenth-century families, their move from village to town represented an abandonment of institutional religion. I was born in 1933 and I cannot remember any of my family (parents, grandparents, uncles or aunts) showing any interest in religious belief or practice. Certainly, none of them attended Church regularly. Yet the conventions of the past remained, and my father was horrified when I drifted into a Methodist Sunday School at six. The aesthetics of religion have always touched my emotions and at that age I thought the polished mahogany and crude mosaics of the Primitive Methodist Church in the Durham mining village where I then lived were the ultimate in beauty, and the annual anniversary service had the touch of heaven. My non-church-going Anglican family viewed non-conformity as dangerous and lower-class, so I was sent to an Anglican Sunday School and confirmed in Newcastle-upon-Tyne in 1946. I soon abandoned church-going and settled down to the normal secular life of my grammar-school contemporaries. In these years after 1945 many of us had a deep interest in politics, but I cannot remember that religion played any prominent part in our discussions. Above all, our life was dominated by the northern creed of advancement. Success in education was supposed to lead to an improvement in life, and material success (through educational achievement) was seen as the main end of existence.

History was then my passion and has remained my main interest. As a child I had adored visiting ancient cathedrals, and increasingly Church history became a fascination. A school contemporary (one of the few religious figures in my school) took me to an Anglo-Catholic High Mass on Corpus Christi Day 1951. I was fascinated, just as John Betjeman was, at this new world of mystery and beauty. At one level it touched all my interest in history and tradition, but it went deeper than that, though it could not be described as a religious conversion. A question mark was placed against all the values and ambitions on which I had hitherto organised my life. For the first time I began to experience mystery and a depth to existence which could not be contained within my northern creed of hard work and success.

It was both puzzling and disturbing and it is a mark of my pragmatic upbringing that I immediately concentrated on hard facts. Truth was a commodity that could be studied and tested, and by reading all that was possible the truth or falsehood of the Christian religion could be discovered. The mystery remained, and the belief that in Jesus we see God, and that in the Holy Communion we share his life, did not respond so easily to the research that had served me so well in my historical studies.

Religion has never been easy for me in that I am not haunted by fear and find much to enjoy and to occupy me in the ordinary business of living. Cambridge in the early 1950s was deeply interested in religion. College Chapels were popular, CICCU thrived, and the Anglo-Catholic churches that I attended were full. My worry was that what I conceived to be religion might just be an attempt to escape materialism and find in 'the beauty of holiness' an antidote to a dull life. The idea of ordination almost began as an attempt to prove committal to myself. The truth was that this feeling of mystery and depth evoked by aesthetic and historical interests was proving to be more disturbing than I either expected or wanted.

The crucial stage in my religious development came when I went to work with UMCA in Africa from 1955 to 1958. The Universities

Mission to Central Africa had been founded in the mid-nineteenth century as a result of the work of Livingstone. It soon developed into the great Anglo-Catholic missionary society of the Church of England. Priests and lay-workers were required to be celibate and were paid £30 a year plus their keep. We lived in simple dried-brick African-style houses and followed a life similar to that of a religious community. There was certainly much to appeal to the romantic – services in thatched churches, unaccompanied singing, all within the mystery of Africa. Yet here I experienced the Divine in such a way that it has never left me. The men and women I worked with showed true holiness in their devotion and dedication. A priest called Donald Parsons had worked at a village named Luatala since the early 1920s. It was a desolate area adjacent to Mozambique. He lived in total simplicity and in the middle of superstition, poverty, and sickness he had created a Christian community. He was totally at one with his people. The Divine was seen in the way that Christian belief changed the whole moral climate. Once I went out to help bring in a leper who had been left in the bush. It was in a remote area and the family, afraid of infection, had placed him in the open to fend for himself with limited help. In such graphic situations, it was possible to see the fulfilment of the Christian ideal that man was created in God's image and that this must guide life. In Africa I learned that life had meaning and purpose only within the context of a living faith. The beauty of holiness was not just a romantic escape but could become an ideal in the world of men. The transformation of the things of the world into the life of God within the Mass became an inspiration and guide to life amid all the problems of a poor, disease-ridden part of Africa. I had touched a reality which would never leave me.

It seemed of crucial importance to affirm this ideal and not to allow it to become just an optional extra to life. I prepared for ordination at Cambridge and was made Deacon in 1959.

Yet my life has never followed the pattern I intended. In 1960 all my thoughts were to return to Africa, but the days of English priests in Africa were approaching their end. In 1962 I was asked to go as Chaplain to Eton. I never thought I had made a decision for life and in fact I told Robert Birley (the Headmaster) that I only envisaged staying two years. In fact, my whole career has been in education in England. The Divine has had to be lived out not amid the direct demands of Africa but in the complex world of a secular and doubting society. Harry Williams once said that the sharing of the cross is in 'facing our inability to do the ideal thing with Christ's own courage and faith'. He went on to say, 'We shall not feel we are doing anything magnificent. Probably we shall feel merely that life appears to be something rather chaotic or worse. But we shall be able to recognise this situation as an important part of our calling as Christians.' This seems very like my experience. More insidious, my life has been comfortable, even successful.

It would certainly have satisfied my father had he lived to see it. There is no doubt that though it has occurred in circumstances which are different from what I expected, my patterns of life have still developed within the context of a belief in God and his sacramental presence in the world. I accept that we are in the end responsible for the use that we make of our talents and power. We are men under authority and the reality of our Lord's life and the Church He created must affect all our decisions and relationships. A great change from what I envisaged when I was at school in Newcastle-upon-Tyne.

Part III

Reflections on Religious Experience

34

The Rev. Dr Edward Norman

In medieval society, and in the baroque age, people had visionary experiences of saints. Theirs was a religious culture in which daily intercessions to the saints, and the expectation of help from them in the details of life, was a permanent reality. In the nineteenth century – an age especially characterised by a cult of devotion to the Virgin – people received experiences of Mary whose resonances are still present within Catholic popular spirituality. Today religious experience has become democratised: people no longer need earthly representations of a heavenly order imagined as being like a feudal court, where access to the sovereign was through a hierarchy of vassals. People now expect to receive direct intimations of the Divine; God himself, as Christ, or as some all-encompassing spiritual presence, is, in consequence, what they believe they experience. It is an age of emotional indulgence. The popular expectation is of emotional enrichment and sustenance: religion is regarded as satisfying if it caters for the requirements of some sort of individual emotional fulfilment. Religion, indeed, is so familiarly expressed as a dimension of personal sensation that many do not find they can believe in it unless it enhances their emotional texture. Knowledge of the saints or of the nature of Christ himself, in fact, is less familiar and less precise in modern society. Reported religious experiences, as a consequence, tend to be more general: God is sensed as a warm presence suffusing the individual with a feeling of spiritual well-being, or he is discerned as a beckoning light, or a confirmation of universal brotherhood. Thus human values and expectations are authenticated by reference to a divine index whose existence simulates (or parodies) worldly hopes of individual significance.

It is all rather suggestively related to the cultural forms and expectations of each age and society. And so it should be in a way, for Christianity was committed by the Saviour to a living tradition, a succession of those who believe in him, and it is thus unavoidably expressed within the shifting and relative cultures through which it passes. There are problems about this, of which the primary one is discovering the criteria for determining what things in the tradition of belief are of permanent value, and what are contingent and so exchangeable in each age and place. The major difficulty about assessment of religious experience, however, relates to the nature of the individual transmission. Why should God choose the people he is claimed to do for these special intimations of his presence? It is evidently a random business. The difficulty is paralleled by the phenomenon of psychical experience. Those who believe they are in touch with the spirits of the dead demonstrate an astonishing discrimination in their chosen means of communication, yet are themselves very randomly selected from human society. The messages transmitted from beyond the grave, furthermore, tend to be of notable triviality, relating to cosy confirmation of worldly attachments, and so forth, whose inconsequence is in stark contrast to the august manner of the communication – nothing less than a suspension of the norms by which all the rest of human experience is directed.

This last point also underlies a difficulty with many reported instances of direct experience of the Divine. God has set up a set of references for human life which, for most people in most cultures, excludes immediate experience of his presence. He is known about through the natural order (through the creation) and through Revelation. The first is discerned by reason, and is universal among thinking creatures, and the second by the adherence of the individual to the tradition of believers who preserve the Revealed truth and who construct and develop its meaning through the successive centuries. The second way is thus the Church of Christ. Why, it is necessary to ask, is God imagined to select some and not others from among the body of the believers to make special and mysterious indications of his presence? This is not a reference to the divine manner, well documented in the Bible, of particular individuals becoming messengers of grace to others, but to the supposition that some Christians receive personal spiritual 'experiences' and some do not. The contemporary assumption that actual experiences of the Divine (the *feelings* people have in worship, or in human relationships conceived as expressions of a 'higher' spiritual dimension) are virtually inseparable from the truth of religion means that for many this will scarcely seem a pertinent question. But that is a very modern view. The fact is that for most people in traditional society there was no such expectation of a personal experience of religious truth. Religion was a collective experience: it was something which defined the identity of a society, even when that society, as with the earliest Christians, was a society within a larger and hostile society. Religion was a learned tradition; it did not rest on individual assent since people were born into it or were compulsorily incorporated into it when the group of which they were a part was itself re-oriented by political or other circumstance. People did not expect to receive any 'holy' feelings, any emotional sustenance, from religious belief in the modern, post-romantic sense. What they expected was actual help with daily labour (through the intercession of the saints), and the gift of salvation from Christ himself. Adherence to the Christian faith meant identification with the general tradition of the believers. It was a matter of loyalty and obligation, a religious counterpart of the systems of allegiance that characterised ancient and medieval society, which was, indeed, made to legitimise them. Actual individual experience of the Divine was so rare as to be truly remarkable. The events concerned, and the lives of the individuals involved, were accordingly treasured. From the modern viewpoint it seems as if there were enormous numbers of them – but that is because centuries of experiences have been compressed in perspective, and what was once unusual and episodic is accordingly made to seem normal and frequent. The 'Age of Faith' was not characterised by direct intimations of the divine presence, but by a confident and nearly universal adherence to religious institutions as the vehicle of personal and social identity.

In the modern world, on the other hand, huge numbers of people report some kind of sense of a divine presence, on specified occasions of their lives. It has to be said, however, that these experiences have a very close relationship to cultural expectations. The pursuit of meaning for life in general, which haunts the secularised and individualised people of modern Western society, and the demand for emotional enrichment may well in some instances suggest a sense of the divine presence which has no reality outside the sensation of the individual recipient. The recent popularity of films about the paranormal has prompted large numbers of apparently paranormal experiences reported by individuals. The human imagination has a great capacity for self-fulfilment. In traditional society, as in some countries of the developing world to this day, religion involves trance-like seizures, visions, miraculous occurrences, and communications with the dead. Testimony to the incidence of these things goes back to the start of the human record. But people see what they want to see, and they experience things which correspond to their emotional expectations. Who can say what is authentic: what is the visitation of a presence that has objective reality? For most people in most cultures, surely, religion should be understood, as once it was, not as a matter of feelings but as a matter of allegiance. Christians are to adhere to Christ. They are to forsake earthly attachments for him – the Scriptural record is very clear about this. They are to be baptised into his death. Their faith, that is to say, is described by identification with his body of believers rather than by internal revelations of a divine scenography.

35

The Rt. Rev. Michael Turnbull

There's more to experience than meets the eye. Standing in front of a great painting the impact greets the senses. It is important to hold on to that. It is personal and unique. But to be enriched and assured the invasion of the senses needs the stimulus of the mind. A knowledgeable friend may expound the technical skills of mixing the paint and applying it to canvas. He may enlarge our vision by describing the artist and the period in which he worked. He provides a critical framework of how others have seen the painting. Gradually the sense experience is taken by our mental faculties into the reflective, interpersonal and intellectual realms. A work of art then begins to form part of a tapestry against which our attitudes are shaped and our perceptions turned into activity. We may understand the painting as part of the development of thought which influences current political or philosophical thinking.

Experience of the divine is dangerous if it relies only on my response. That leads to blind fanaticism. If it remains subjective, the God in me, internalised or part of a personally constructed defence against the unanswerable, then the experience becomes self-defeating. At the other extreme it is possible to be coldly objective and too analytical about our experiences – searching only for the transcendent, something out there. To perceive experience as only having integrity if it can in some way be verified is to lose its immediacy and personal application.

These two responses to experience can perhaps be paralleled by the distinction made by William James between the religion of healthy-mindedness and the religion of the sick soul. James related these categories to once-born and twice-born religion. About the same time Soderblom distinguished between personality-asserting and personality-denying religious experience or the religion of revelation and the religion of redemption. The contemporary emergence of creation spirituality (see the works of Matthew Fox) continues the same divisions.

The truth is that both types of religious experience need each other and they are not mutually exclusive. As Hans Kung has said, 'reflection' (by which he means intellectualism and pragmatism) 'lives by experience' and 'experience needs the critical illumination and assurance of reflection'. It is against that background that I must revert to the first person. In my experience there are four words which bridge the dichotomy between the subjective and objective, between that which comes from within and that which invades, between the reality of sin and life affirmation.

The first word is *energy*. I detect within me a life force which is sustained by and responds to the whole of creation. It is real in itself and provides meaning and purpose without which life would be intolerable. It finds its true verification in meaning rather than empirical proof. But it is incomplete and unsustainable without outside resource. In Christian terms the dynamic between inner experience and outward resources is reflected in the nature of the divine itself. The hidden Creator is made known by the revelation by the Son and made available by the power of the Spirit.

This interaction within the Divine is mirrored in pragmatic terms by the need of individual experience to be nourished by community. My personal experience of this began by contact with the lay community at Scargill in Yorkshire. Here the combination of natural beauty, revelation by Biblical teaching and the disciplines of community life provided a wholeness of experience which was formative for me. Since then I have discovered that family life, team work and explorations into the Celtic and Benedictine traditions have been the settings in which the divine energy has been released.

The second word is *light*. What is it that has gradually changed my seeing, in common with the rest of humanity, into my perceiving in a personal and unique way without losing my bonds with all other human beings? My answer is 'The Light of the World'. All of His illumination is shed on the world, but within that are the lights lit within my life in my time and place. All of it is 'given', but some of it is 'taken' by me as an act of volition and commitment. So fickle is my will that the experience is often negligible, but there is enough of it sometimes to suggest that He has given me light to see things as He sees them. My response is praise and adoration that in His light I see light – in the natural world, in humankind, in self-perception.

The third word is *wounds*. If experiencing the Divine is about reality, then that experience must discover some meaning in the wounds of the world. My pain at the suffering and horrors around us is due partly to my accountable sin and partly to the divine pain. My experience of the Divine is painful because in it I recognise the Divine experiences me. And just at the point where that becomes unacceptable I have to acknowledge that I am acceptable – wounds and all. That experience is shallow, wishful thinking and, for me, extremely irresponsible, unless the place where I experience it is at the Cross of Christ. His wounds make mine a reality. His wounds also make it possible to live with mine. There is no place where the experience of the Divine is more real – or more necessary. Michael Ramsey said: '... the Christian puts himself deliberately into the presence of God with the needs and sorrows of humanity upon his heart.'

The final word is *doubt*, which may seem a strange note with which to conclude. Yet it seems to me to be in the nature of all experience to have the courage to be wrong. Anyone who claims that their experience contains all truth is a danger to the world and especially to his neighbour. There is always the lingering doubt that this or that experience, however profound, may be the manufacture of some egoistic, self-preserving corner of our being. To be certain, beyond all doubt, that at last we have arrived is the most deceptive experience of all.

The experience of the Divine is never a completion. A mountain peak is the best vantage point from which to see many horizons. They beckon us – not to fulfil sensuous desires for more and more experience – but to hold the promise of energy and light, though the path may take us through the valleys of wounds and doubt. This pilgrimage of divine exploration is well expressed by J.J. Balfour:

> Our highest truths are but half-truths.
> Think not to settle down forever in any truth.
> Make use of it as a tent in which to pass a summer's night,
> But build no house of it, or it will be your tomb.
> When you first have an inkling of its insufficiency
> And begin to descry a dim counter-truth looming up beyond,
> Then weep not, but give thanks,
> It is the Lord's voice whispering: 'Take up thy bed and walk.'

36

The Rt. Rev. Michael Ball

Oscar Wilde was purported to have said 'Prayer should never be answered. If it is, it becomes mere correspondence.' Hidden behind his flippancy was a truth, as with most flippant remarks, that is difficult to express in other ways. Hidden behind it is the truth that there is an in-built inequality about the encounter with the Divine in prayer, and perhaps its chief wonder, its incredibility, is that prayer is possible at all. Hidden behind that saying is the fact that prayer is not principally some divine human swapping of requests, though in his unbelievable humility God always allows our askings, and gives us the privilege of our hopes. Hidden behind Wilde's epigram is a feeling that prayer has an ordinariness about it, a normality, even if letter-exchanging is not a top-priority feature. We have a God who stoops low enough to allow that ordinariness of communication.

So for me almost my major wonder in the divine encounter we call prayer is the humility of God; the wonder of that prayerful revealing of his nature to mere mortals; the fact that prayer can be described at all as an exploration into the nature of God. That's quite incredible. Not only that: if we consider that public worship is also a form of prayer, that shared intimacy becomes yet more amazing. Amazing that God's humility allows us that contact through the words of Scripture. Through writings which, however inspired, are words of men and women culturally conditioned, historically formed. Even the words of his Son express the divine humility, the divine truth, by being so conditioned. Amazing that in God's lowliness he should allow the things of an evolved creation to express and carry that prayerful intimacy; bread and wine, water, a ring of gold, a smear of oil. Word and Sacraments are expressions of God's desire for the whole creation; yet he will not crush so much as a blade of grass, as Kierkegaard says, in that foolish desire in the tip-toeing of his humility.

Let me enlarge on that theme in two ways. Let me use two simple schemes, one my own, one often used when young and old are taught to pray. I often describe prayer, Sunday-school-like, in four words beginning with the letter 'S'. First, prayer is a skill. We have to learn it, practise it, have set times, set postures perhaps, and so on. Now I realise that part of that is because of our human weakness, our human blockages, our human distractions that prevent clarity of vision. We have to keep at it if we are to get closer to our aweful companion. But the wonder is that God allows it to be so. Allows us to treat him almost as a musical instrument, which by practice will yield music that is ever more beautiful, yet often more distantly beguiling. Somewhere in that allowing lies a humility that could only be divine. The humility that allows us to govern the time, and to construct the notes. That prayer should be a skill at all is a lowliness in that, by taking us forward by degrees, God realises, in his love, that should he reveal himself, unfold his nature too suddenly, we would be overwhelmed and unable to stand the beauty.

But prayer should also be a state. Used in both senses of that word; a country and a condition. Obviously there are moments of special nearness, but it is also a perpetual state. Just as a married couple are in the married state all the time, not just when they are in physical nearness, so with our state of prayer. In the same way as a monk is in the religious state whether he is worshipping or sinning. It is incredible that God should allow this to be so. Prayer in a sense is the marriage of our nature to God's nature, and that he should stay in that state of intimacy whatever our condition, whatever we are doing or saying, awake or asleep, passes comprehension. I sometimes also describe prayer as giving God permission to act. It is his commitment to this union, this state of being with us wherever, whatever, that allows him to act in his world. This prayerful co-mingling that is a permanent co-mingling enables God to flood the world with his presence. It enables God to unite those two states, those two countries. That is amazing.

I press on. My third 'S' is sharing. Prayer is also a sharing. This is particularly so in intercession, obviously. We all spend a fair amount of time bombarding the Almighty with requests on our own and others' behalf. I become, however, more and more uncertain about what I am actually doing, let alone the how of what I am about. It is strange that prayer is so often thought of for the most part in intercessary terms, despite the fact that theologically, let alone practically, intercessions are the most complex form of prayer we indulge in, and 'indulge in' is the right phrase in some places I visit! I wonder if you remember that verse in the old version of one of the psalms that says, 'One deep, answereth to another because of the noise of the water-pipes.' For me that is as close as I can get to a definition and description of intercession. One deep, our depths answering to God's depths, because of some practical need. (In this case the temple plumbing, perhaps.) Intercession is our heart beating with God's heart; a sharing of depths through practical needs and agonies. But it is also another type of sharing. As I've said, I get asked to take on an enormous number of prayer requests, and some I just throw at God, in the form of a great list, but with others I try to do some 'alongsideness' at depth. I try to be in the hospital bed beside the patient awaiting an operation, and imaginatively share the fear and phobias. I try to sit alongside that Ethiopian mother with a starving child in the desert; sharing her terror as much as I can. In that way we somehow work with the God who is there also. There alongside his wounded children with his own depths of woundedness. Again, what humility, *humi* to be 'on the ground' with his people.

Let me put one more 'S' before you and then turn to something different. Prayer should have style. It should be our own style as much as our own nose; our expressions are ours alone. It should be that by which we are recognised. There is a tendency to over-borrow. To use the Franciscan way on Monday perhaps; the Ignation method on Tuesday; the Dame Julian meditational approach on Wednesday, ending with a nervous breakdown probably on Thursday! But eventually we have to find our own style, however much prayer-plagiarising we do along the way. It is right and proper that we should. They are after all master and mistresses of prayer. Our style, however, is a gift which God in his humility has given us so that we can reveal his kaleidoscopic nature through his kaleidoscopic creation. In this way prayer becomes part of our total make-up. It becomes almost physical as well as spiritual and mental, and hence a creative revealing of God's humanity.

Four 'S's to push up the roadway of prayer-revealing. They are signs of the way God enters silently and gently into and through his creation to mould it to his love and purpose.

A.C.T.S.

Let me speedily put another scheme in front of you and then turn it on its head. We were told in our Confirmation cradles no doubt that prayer has four parts: Adoration, Confession, Thanksgiving and Supplication. They even represented, we were told sadly, a sort of hierarchy, Adoration being near the summit of our prayerful Mount Carmel. Of course Adoration does humble us and hone us to the heavenly. Confession, whether to a priest, or generally in church, or to our eiderdown at night, does reveal our inmost being. It reveals some of the things that too often direct our course. Thanksgiving, too, is a realisation of God's mercy and care, and our perpetual need to realise it if we are to be fashioned to his likeness. St Augustine distinguishes in this way between creating and fashioning ('Thou hast made me and fashioned me'). And I have already said more than enough about supplication or intercession.

For me, however, the amazing thing is that it is God who really illustrates those acts and so often tells us so in prayer and worship, and most of all in his incarnation. Take Adoration. God adores his creation so much that he becomes part of it. Imitation is the sincerest form of flattery. God does not merely imitate his creation but actually enters it. What surpassing adoration is that? As I said, Confession is a revealing of our underlying nature and motives. God does exactly that in Christ. Christ is God's confession to mankind. In him we see God's underlying nature and his motives of love. God makes his confession, agonisingly so, in Christ. Likewise, Thanksgiving. So thankful is God for us, so *over the top* is this gratitude, that he actually takes our humanity into the Trinity at the Ascension. We sit at God's right hand as expressions of his adoration and thanksgiving for us. Finally, Christ is, of course, God's Supplication. He beseeches us to be like him. he is our intercession pattern in his energy, his artistry, his wounds, and himself.

So there are some patterns of God's humility and our mutual praying. Dame Julian suggests that when Christ accepts our prayers, which he always does, and does cheerfully, 'He sends it up above, and puts it in the treasury where it will never perish. There it remains continually before God and his holy ones, ever helping our needs. And when we come to our bliss, it will be given back to us, as a contribution to our joy with his eternal, glorious gratitude.'

So let me end where I began. In all this wordy description of the divine human encounter in prayer it is the humility of God that overwhelms us. For in that divine human encounter is, in the end, an encounter, a secret swapping within the Holy Trinity itself. That God should not only allow us into that swapping, but in some incredible way allow us to influence it, is humility indeed. So much so that the obligation, the command to pray is in the end only fulfilled in our hesitation to do so at all.

37

The Rev. Professor Christopher Rowland

Some identifiable experience distinguishable from the ordinariness of existence is believed to mark the moment when the divine confronts us in our experience. Religious experience is special, peculiar, perhaps at times somewhat spooky. Above all it is best found when unsullied by the exigencies of everyday life. Surely that must be the case? What else can be fitting for the divine power which transcends all we can understand or see? It is a view which has its attractions. And yet it seems to me to miss the heart of experience of God: its very ordinariness. We view mystics with awe and perhaps some envy. They have been privileged to have a divine visitation. In both Judaism and Christianity the goal of the mystical quest is the vision of God, the beatific vision. That great reality is shut off from us. We may hope to see it on the Last Day, but only a spiritual elite may hope to anticipate it. But there is another version of the beatific vision which is central to my understanding of religious experience.

In the Gospel of Matthew (25:31ff) the heavenly son of man sits on the throne of glory; the mystical appearance of the divine judge finally confronts the nations. This eschatological appearance of the glorious heavenly son of man is no remote expectation confined to an eschatological future. In 25:35ff we find the interpretation of the glorious theophany in the more mundane circumstances of human need. Thus, surprising as it may seem to them, the righteous learn that they have in fact already met the son of man who occupies the throne of glory in the persons of the naked, the poor, the hungry, the stranger and the prisoner. The moment of judgement is brought into the present and its outcome determined by patterns of reaction to those who appear to be not worth noticing. They are told, 'As you have done it to one of the least of these you have done it to me.' Here is the classic example of entertaining strangers unawares. It turns out to be the moment when the Lord of the Universe appears to receive one's ministrations.

Even if we are not justified in seeing the hungry, the thirsty and the rest of the outcasts as an embodiment of the heavenly son of man, the relationship between them is surely very close. They are an extension of the person of the heavenly figure. The language which is used at the end of this judgement scene echoes that earlier in the gospel:

receiving the disciple and the child means receiving Jesus (10:42; 18:5). Behind these formulae lies the Jewish concept of agency in which the representative acts with plenipotentiary powers on behalf of the sender. So the vision of the one throned in glory is located also among the outcast and not merely in heaven on the last day.

The prospect of final judgement meets all humanity in persons we might prefer to neglect. It is a telling reminder that religious experience is not the warm feeling within or the satisfaction of stimulating worship or preaching, however spine-tingling and illuminating. When that is cut off from the practice of righteousness it has forfeited the right to be religious experience. It is an empty shell, just like the Temple which Ezekiel saw with the divine glory having fled from it. The beggar on the street, the refugee, the ill-treated peasant or the 'untouchable' cannot be accepted as a fact of life as far as experience of God is concerned. One meets in the poor, the outcast and the vulnerable none other than the representative of the Judge of the world.

We may find ourselves responding by asking, 'How may I respond adequately to such need?' The practice of charity requires of us our imagination, our co-operation and our attentiveness. Our imagination demands of us the ability to see beyond the horizons of our concerns to other peoples and places. Our attentiveness is required to use our eyes to see what is really happening in our midst. Those who entertained angels unawares did so because they were not wrapped up in themselves. The voice of God was heeded, and the request for bread did not fall on deaf ears. Yet the whole earth is full of God's glory, not only in what we take to be majesty but in the identification with the lowly. So we may look in vain for the Judge of the world and fail to catch a glimpse of God standing before us in the immediacy of need. There will be many ways of responding. Some may be more immediate; others of a more collective kind. For those whose lot is one of privilege and power it may be necessary, as Dietrich Bonhoeffer said of the role of the Church in the face of Jewish persecution (echoing the words of Proverbs 31:8), to 'speak for those who cannot speak for themselves'.

Religious experience is not 'for me' alone; it is about myself in relationship to 'the other':

> If someone says 'I love God', while at the same time hating a brother or sister, that one is a liar. If they do not love their brother or sister whom they have seen, they are incapable of loving God they have not seen (I John 4:19f).

To meet the poor and the vulnerable is to be reminded of our own deepest need, so painful that we are prepared to shut out any reminder of it in the faces of others. Yet our quest for wholeness requires us to take both seriously and not imagine that we can survive by neglecting either. The vulnerable person demands attention, compassion and action, just as the needy other part of each one of us cries out from the depths. Both protest against patterns of 'adult' reasonableness which justify structures which protect from suffering and need, thereby excluding, impoverishing and silencing. The God within and without will not have it so and demands a hearing.

We may respond by erecting ways of defending ourselves against God in the fond belief that we are protecting the divine glory. We want to build our tabernacles to encapsulate the divine glory much as Peter did on the Mount of Transfiguration. Thereby we hope to repeat the experience again and again. But the glory departs to unexpected and uncomfortable places. Our sacred spaces and actions then can become ends in themselves, so easily cut off from life. So we imagine holiness to be so special that we cannot contaminate it by the drabness of human need. Isaiah learnt differently. The call of the holy God in a sacred place turned his eyes to the iniquities committed to the poor and the outcast outside the confines of the Holy Place. God demanded of him a conversion. There could be no satisfaction with the experience of the One high and lifted up, for the gaze had to be fixed elsewhere in the stuff of society and politics. There is no reason to suppose that religious experience is to be any different for us.

38

The Rev. Canon Eric James

It was at the seventieth birthday party of Diana Collins, the widow of Canon John Collins – erstwhile Dean of Oriel and Canon of St Paul's and founder of Christian Action – that Trevor Huddleston, who had been reading my *Life of Bishop John A.T. Robinson*, made the kind observation that he would much like me to write his biography. 'But,' he added, 'I'm not having one written while I'm alive.' I rather approved of that; but I did not see why we shouldn't meet regularly, so that I could at least begin the task, and perhaps preserve memories which might otherwise be lost. So, for the last four years, Bishop Trevor and I have met, roughly every six weeks, for a meal and a talk together.

But what has happened as I have got on with the work is that I have realised – as I did when writing the biography of John Robinson – that you cannot write a life of such a person without confronting some taxing questions of theology, spirituality, and faith in relation to life – without, in other words, 'experiencing the Divine'.

Here are just a few examples.

In a post-Freudian age, a biographer is bound to pay particular attention to his subject's infancy and childhood. Trevor Huddleston maintains he had an 'idyllic' childhood: seeing little of his parents – who were in India much of the time – until he was twelve, but being brought up by a wealthy widowed aunt. But he also describes in graphic detail his imaginary companion, whom he called by the rather odd name 'Gilkert'. He played with him and talked with him, rather as Jung used to talk with his fantasy-figure Philemon. Trevor retained a very vivid mental picture of Gilkert: a wraith-like, wispy figure, with fair, almost white, hair.

I cannot myself believe that an 'idyllic' childhood and such a figure sort well together. Such a figure surely betokens an inner aloneness, at least at that time. But one is not surprised to encounter in later years a somewhat reclusive person. And as one ponders Trevor the man of prayer – and from his youth onwards his disciplined daily prayer is one of his most notable characteristics – one is bound to ask how much that prayer is essentially an extension, development and transmuting of his relationship with his childhood companion.

A second area of questioning arises for me in the realm of Trevor's vocation and calling. Trevor from an early age felt called to the priesthood; and, indeed, when his sister, four years older than himself, was confirmed in St Paul's, Bedford, by Bishop Furse of St Albans, resplendent in cope, Trevor clearly remembers looking at him in wonder and saying to himself: 'I am going to be a bishop.' From his Oxford years he felt called to be a monk.

When you write the biography of someone like Trevor, you cannot avoid pressing the direct question: 'Does God call particular people to a particular work?' And, what precisely does that mean? Is it a fairly isolated phenomenon? Does he call only men – and people who have been to places like Lancing College and Christ Church? Or does he call men – and women – from the housing estates of Stepney and the villages of Masasi? The phenomenon of the able-bodied Trevor, during the Second World War, resisting call-up to the armed forces, because God had called him to be a monk, is worthy of our attention. It meant more to Trevor than a simple statement that to be a monk was the best way of using his gifts. He meant what he said. He believed God had called him, and called him then to test his vocation to the Community of the Resurrection, Mirfield, Yorkshire.

It is, of course, easy to be wise after the event: after looking at the way Trevor was used in South Africa and Central Africa, and to say: 'Clearly God called and empowered him.' Certainly his gifts have been hugely used. Shakespeare assures us that 'there's a special providence in the fall of a sparrow'. In Trevor's case you need to believe there was a special providence in his being on duty as Servitor at Mirfield when Raymond Raynes returned from South Africa to be Superior of the Community: even a special providence in Raymond's sickness when his ship came home – for without that Raymond and Trevor would probably never have had the conversations which caused Raymond to make Trevor his successor in South Africa.

Another area of experience of the divine arises with the remarkable transformation that took place in Trevor once he had got to South Africa: the change from Trevor the recluse to Trevor the scourge of apartheid: from Trevor obedient to authority to Trevor the reformer and, indeed, the revolutionary. In a sense, the scandal of the situation that greeted him is sufficient to account for the change in him. Indelible in his memory were the words of Basil Jellicoe he had heard as a boy of twelve from the pulpit of All Saints', Margaret Street: 'Slums are the outward and visible sign of an inward and spiritual disgrace.' But something psychophysical seems to have happened to Trevor. It is more than just a guess to say that the affection physically expressed, which Trevor received daily from the children of Sophiatown, effected that change. Archbishop Desmond Tutu has written recently: 'If Trevor wore a white cassock, it did not remain clean for long, as he trudged the dusty streets of Sophiatown, with little urchins and grubby fingers always waiting to touch him, and calling out "Fader" with obvious affection in their little voices. He loved us – tremendous! He was fond of letting you sit on his lap, and in 1978, when I told people at the Lambeth Conference that I used to sit on Trevor's lap, they looked at me, looking so decrepit, and him still very sprightly, and I don't think they believed me.'

One of the most crucial areas of 'experience of the Divine' in Trevor's life was through his relations with the Archbishop of Cape Town, Geoffrey Clayton, who had first been his Bishop in Johannesburg. Both were enemies of apartheid; but Clayton was a gradualist, Huddleston more of an absolutist.

Clayton was undoubtedly a good and holy man, but he believed it was the duty of the Church in South Africa to resist the Government of South Africa to the point of breaking the law only if the State prevented black and white *worshipping* together. Trevor believed that to protest only when black and white were forbidden to *worship* together and not to protest when they were forbidden to *live* together was pietism.

It has to be said that when the South African Government brought in a bill that would prevent mixed worship, Clayton gathered the bishops together and said he would go to prison rather than agree to such a measure. They spent Shrove Tuesday and Ash Wednesday 1957 drafting a letter to the Government. Having signed and posted the letter, Clayton believed he might indeed be arrested; but that fateful day on which the anxious Clayton put his signature to the letter he had a heart attack and died.

Not only the Archbishop of Cape Town, but the Archbishop of Canterbury, Geoffrey Fisher, told Huddleston that his methods were wrong. But of the three only Trevor had *lived* in a native location. And Trevor could never forget the words of Frank Weston, Bishop of Zanzibar, to the Anglo-Catholic Congress of 1923: 'You cannot claim to worship Jesus in the tabernacle if you do not pity Jesus in the slum ... It is folly, it is madness, to suppose that you can worship Jesus in the Sacrament and Jesus on the throne of glory, when you are sweating Him in the bodies and souls of His children.'

It is curious that Trevor Huddleston, son of Captain Sir Ernest Whiteside Huddleston, Commander of the Royal Indian Navy, should be sent out as a *white* priest – with little training for the job – to be priest-in-charge of a parish of 80,000 *black* people; and, just when every white civil servant was preparing to leave Tanganyika, should become the white bishop of an overwhelmingly *black* diocese? There seems to me here a kind of consecrated imperialism: the kind of imperialism that found money for the education of this individual and that in Masasi, for hospitals, for schools for the blind, and so on. At the end of an era of paternalism 'Father' Huddleston, rejecting as utterly offensive the description of black Africans as 'children' and working with and alongside black leaders, and treating them as equals, retained nevertheless not only paternal but paternalist attitudes in conforming himself to a paternalist system. Trevor could compromise when the Gospel demanded it.

His enthusiastic support for the policies and politics of President Nyerere and the Arusha declaration was based on Christian convictions and principles; yet when one sees the dismal state of Tanzania's economy, as I have seen it recently in Masasi, there are questions that cannot be avoided. By the Church in the person of Trevor endorsing State policies, were these policies promoted for longer than would otherwise have been the case? In Tanzania today, exports have collapsed: roads, schools and hospitals are in a parlous state; transport is chaotic; and the country has become dependent on aid. Agriculture, the mainstay of the Tanzanian economy, has suffered from political programmes and policies. Above all, the loss of incentives has caused the decline in production. Moral exhortation to produce for the collective good has been shown to be no substitute for material incentives – in Tanzania as in Eastern Europe. By the 1980s many of Nyerere's original ideas were corrupted. The party had become a means of controlling the people. The urban educated elite were imposing their ideology on the rural peasantry. Corruption and inefficiency had become the norm.

All this has to be set against considerable social and political achievements. There is a genuine pride in nationhood in Tanzania which transcends tribal differences: an uncommon thing in Africa. Tanzanians point out that they have been at peace since independence. So although significant improvements in health in Masasi Diocese since Bishop Trevor's time are as hard to find as improvements in the *quality* of education, there have been huge – if unquantifiable – benefits from the Nyerere years; and Bishop Trevor only did what any prophet and conscientious Christian leader would have done in giving President Nyerere his full support.

Trevor Huddleston is often portrayed as inflexible. Certainly at first, having been brought up as a rather sectarian Anglo-Catholic, he was for many years opposed to that first fruit of the Ecumenical

Movement, the Church of South India. But in the later years of his ministry he had been much involved in the latest and most radically ecumenical movement: that which is concerned with the mutual understanding of the major world religions. Meeting, for instance, Muslims and working with them – in South Africa, Masasi, Mauritius and Madagascar – the sectarian Anglo-Catholic ceased to have institutional Christianity as his chief concern and has become more Catholic in its profoundest sense: concerned with the universal.

Similarly, at the outset of his ordained ministry he was utterly opposed to the ordination of women, but in his later years he has seen clearly that there is more than one apartheid in this world: not least that which makes of women a 'lesser breed without the law'. Those who speak of the inflexibility of Trevor usually mean that he is inflexibly anti-apartheid. He would gladly plead guilty to that.

No one who knows Trevor Huddleston intimately can deny one fact: that he is in a rather old-fashioned sense a man of God. Living in a few rooms at the top of the vicarage of St James's, Piccadilly, he looks for all the world like a solitary, and there is still much of the monk about him. He not only maintains his prayer and spiritual discipline: prayer remains the very centre of his life.

But 'for all the world' is not an unimportant phrase. Close to Piccadilly Circus, he is available to the media and to such leaders of the world as seek him out: people like Julius Nyerere, Nelson Mandela, Sonny Ramphal. And, if they press him, he will fly to the ends of the earth. He is undoubtedly a man of God – at God's disposal – and therefore a man of and for the world.

It is surely one of the most remarkable facts of our time that after all that the black people of South Africa have suffered, it was a white Christian bishop whom the ANC asked to open their first conference in freedom.

When I ask myself *why* they made Trevor their choice, it is, again, Archbishop Tutu who I think provides the best answer. He says: 'I was in hospital for twenty months with TB, and if Father Huddleston was in Johannesburg he made it a point to visit me at least once a week during those twenty months. I was just a nonentity, thirteen years old, and yet he paid so much attention to me.' 'And,' he adds, almost as an afterthought, 'you could have knocked me down with a feather, young as I was at the time, when this man doffed his hat to my mother. I couldn't understand a white man doffing his hat to a black woman, an *uneducated* black woman.'

It may not be easy but it is undoubtedly a privilege to write the life of such a man. For me, it undoubtedly means experiencing the Divine.

39

The Very Rev. Michael Mayne

To speak of religious experience is to speak of mystery, but to speak, in the first instance, of that which is natural. My religious experience – better, my spiritual experience – arises from my humanness. It becomes possible because I am an embodied spirit, knowing what it is to love and to be loved, capable of moments when I am made aware of the mystery of a transcendent 'otherness' in myself, in people, and in the world about me, so that I am (however briefly) taken out of myself, losing myself in wonder.

Of course I can only claim to experience one mystery at first hand: that I exist at all and that I exist as *me*. I am this flawed but mysteriously embodied spirit, 'fearfully and wonderfully made', creative, imaginative, curious, able to laugh at myself and to empathise with the mystery that is you; able to speculate, to fall in love; able so to communicate my invisible thoughts and ideas by 'incarnating' them in words that they can strike a chord in others' own different but shared experience of reality. I can give my attention equally to what lies outside me and what lies within me. I can feel a sense of awe. I am able to conceive of things being different from the way they are, to repent and to hope. And beneath it all there lies what I can only describe as a kind of yearning, a hunger, a sense of incompleteness, a deep need to love and to know myself accepted, loved and valued, that may be largely, but is not completely, fulfilled by those who are dearest to me. This too is a mystery.

I am convinced that the whole of creation is a sacrament of God's presence and every human being made in God's likeness and therefore to be seen as holy, though always caught between the 'now' and the 'not yet'. From a host of examples I would choose William Golding's description of a human hand in his novel *Darkness Visible*. The hero, Sim, meets a man who takes his hand and begins to examine it and read the palm.

> Sim was slightly disconcerted by this ... but then he began to look into his own palm, pale, crinkled, the volume, as it were, most delicately bound in this rarest or at least most expensive of all binding material – and then he fell through into an awareness of his own hand that stopped

time in its revolution. The palm was exquisitely beautiful, it was made of light. It was precious and preciously inscribed with a sureness and delicacy beyond art and grounded somewhere else in absolute health. In a convulsion unlike anything he had ever known, Sim stared into the gigantic world of his own palm and saw that it was holy.

What does Blake say? 'To hold infinity in the palm of your hand.'

All spiritual experience stems from the suspicion that I am *this* sort of person (and, therefore, so is everybody else). G.K. Chesterton once wrote of how, following a period of depression, he was granted an insight into himself he never forgot:

> At the back of our brains, so to speak, there is a forgotten blaze or burst of astonishment at our own existence. The object of the artistic and spiritual life is to dig for this sunrise of wonder.

Like most people, I have known startling moments when, moved by beauty or emotion, the world seems illuminated and there is a shift in one's perception of things. Usually these experiences of wonder come in flashes, not consciously sought – but I have to be paying attention. Sometimes they come in a heightened awareness of the natural world and its almost heart-breaking beauty and extravagantly rich variety in which no two snowflakes are alike. Small epiphanies when, in the words of James Joyce's Stephen Dedalus, 'the soul of the commonest object seems to us radiant'. Wordsworthian moments of

> ... objects recognised
> In flashes, and with glory not their own.

Sometimes these small epiphanies come in other, less dramatic, forms. Sometimes, when sharing the joys and sadnesses of others, I have momentarily glimpsed, both in what individuals can endure and in their ability to bring good out of evil, people's quality and their mystery. Sometimes these moments of wonder come in worship, most often for me in the give-and-take, the breaking and the sharing, of the Eucharist. Sometimes in the concert hall or the theatre. Or in the silence of that prayerful looking and waiting we call contemplation.

One thing is sure. Any such experience, like any work of art, is self-evident. It may be deeply subjective, but it feels for a moment like recognising people and objects for what they truly are: it feels like coming home. And yet it is utterly down-to-earth and always within the kaleidoscope of the nitty-gritty of daily life. I believe that God enables us to use the material world as a means of finding him. As R.S. Thomas writes in his poem, 'Emerging':

> We are beginning to see
> now it is matter is the scaffolding
> of spirit …
> it is the plain facts and natural happenings
> that conceal God and reveal him to us
> little by little under the mind's tooling.

Harry Williams' words, with which he introduced his first published book of sermons, still ring true:

> I resolved that I would not preach about any aspect of Christian belief unless it had become part of my own life-blood. … All I could speak of were those things which I had proved to be true in my own experience by living them and by knowing them at first hand.

Spiritual experience does not stand in contrast to our daily experience of the world. On the contrary: it is born of a proper sense of wonder at what lies all about us and within us, the awareness that our lives begin and end in mystery, and that mystery touches our lives at every point.

But I have to move on from what is simply natural. For I can only account for this hunger of the spirit I sometimes feel if it is true that life is the gift of a loving Creator, and that I am created with the sole purpose of learning to respond to him with love, of becoming what I truly am. Part of my experience bears out this truth: part denies it utterly.

The darkness is too close, the evil too sickeningly real. The Holocaust and the cancer cell. The terrorist bomb and the black depression. The experience of sickness or pain or bereavement can make even our most transfigured moments seem no more than a self-deluding, selfish indulgence, powerless to affect the depth of anguish we may feel in the face of darkness. Then we resort to language that Flaubert likened to 'a cracked kettle on which we beat out tunes for bears to dance to, when all the time we are longing to move the stars to pity'. Which is why even the most rewarding experiences of natural religion are ultimately impotent. And why I look to the God disclosed in Christ.

I have had no sudden, blinding conversion, no shattering moments when the earth moved. While the Damascus Road Company make their bids in conversion experiences, not holding such dazzling trumps in my hand, I pass. For me, God has not shown himself in such a dramatic way as to leave no room for doubt; what attracts me, a naturally somewhat guarded soul, is his awesome reticence, leaving room for faith and affirming my freedom. No magic, then; a sign or two, certainly, but no miracles. No proofs or knock-down arguments. Yet I would confess a more profound mystery and claim (with Paul Tillich) the amazed discovery that 'here and there in the world and now and then in ourselves is a New Creation, usually hidden, but sometimes manifest, and certainly manifest in Jesus who is called the Christ'. And chiefly, and most mysteriously and powerfully, made manifest in his Cross. Only a God who, out of love, chooses to communicate with us in our terms and in our language – in words and actions that speak a universal and timeless language: self-giving love, compassion, forgiveness, life-through-death – only such a God will do. In Dietrich Bonhoeffer's words from his Nazi prison cell: 'Only a suffering God can help.'

As a Christian my head-knowledge tells me that my experience of the world's darkness only makes sense if God is Christlike, that undergirding and illuminating this chancy, totally unpredictable creation there is the profound mystery of the God whose 'heart' was once disclosed in Christ. An incarnate God strung up on a cross, who suffered and suffers for his world, his nature revealed as costly love.

As a man, my task has been to test that claim in my experience; to link head-knowledge to heart-knowledge. Like any priest I have celebrated both the joys and the sorrows of human life; in terms of the latter I have sat with the dying, tried to console the bereaved, spent hour upon hour encouraging the unloved and listening to the wounded and the lonely. I have also known the dereliction of a long, debilitating illness, when it was almost impossible to pray at all. And all I know is that, for me, the only words that have helped have had to do with Christ crucified (or rather, the Easter Christ who still bears in his hands the marks of the nails and the wound in his side). The only words that I sense have helped others have had to do with the concept of the suffering God, whose love for each of us cannot be altered or diminished, and of whom I can say with the psalmist:

> If I reach up to heaven thou art there: if I go down to hell thou art there also.

The poet Thomas Blackburn has described how he once found a large crucifix fallen under a slide of scree in the Alps and took the worm-eaten figure back to his home where it hangs on the wall of his dining-room. The poem ends:

> Because it says nothing reasonable
> It explains nothing away,
> And just by gazing into darkness
> Is able to mean more than words can say.

It is a cliché that for some of us the older we get the less intellectual luggage we need to cling to, and the more stubbornly we hold to a few transforming truths – I guess those whose truth has been borne out by our experience and whose validity it would be as foolish to deny as to deny that grass is green and whisky intoxicating. There have been enough times when I have found, as a 'steward of the mysteries', that 'here and there in the world and now and then in ourselves is a New Creation, usually hidden, but sometimes manifest and certainly manifest in Jesus who is called the Christ'. I have scented a different reality that has to do with God, a destination I can only glimpse in this life, both like yet unlike my profoundest human experiences; though self-giving love when I spot it in others is, I guess, the best clue I'll get.

And because the ever-creative God is in all this, *and* the constantly-redeeming God whom I know in Christ is in it too, *and* the Holy Spirit whose task is to open our eyes, then the 'here and there and now and then' moments are the truly valid, authentic moments; and what I know (or at the least *sense*) at these times about the truth of my life in God and his life in me is equally true, I dare to hope, of every moment of my life, both here and hereafter.

40

The Rev. Professor Robin Gill

We hear much today about the problem of evil and the difficulties that this causes those of us who believe in a loving God. I am sure that it is right that we *should* take the problem of innocent suffering (as it is more accurately termed) seriously. However, we hear rather less today about the problem of goodness and the difficulties that this causes those who do not believe in a loving God.

The problem is simply this. Is it rational to be good in ways that go beyond our self-interest unless we believe in a loving God? Surely nobody needs to be persuaded of the power of self-interest. Goodness which coincides wholly with self-interest causes few intellectual problems. Rather it is goodness in a broken world – goodness that is altruistic – that is problematic in a sceptical age. But for me, goodness beyond self-interest offers crucial clues about experiencing the Divine.

Let me illustrate this. When Terry Waite was finally released there was much relief and joy in the country. 'Thank God it is over at last' and 'Thank God he is safe' were expressions I heard again and again. But very soon relief began to be overtaken by more cynical voices. 'He only went there in the first place to boost his own ego.' 'He was really a spy for the CIA.' 'He just wanted to become famous.'

Of course, people of faith should be the first to admit that moral actions are always tainted by self-interest. Practising Christians are reminded of this at every act of worship. Even when we try very hard to be good, the sins of pride and self-interest intervene. We start to feel good that we are being good – and we know that that is not good at all.

Yet to admit that our moral actions are always tainted by self-interest, is not to agree that we can *only* act out of self-interest. What the cynical voices seemed to find difficult to believe was that Terry Waite could have reasons other than pure self-interest for acting as he did. Yet in that very moving television interview which he gave soon after his release, he rightly insisted that he did. He had seen hostages suffering. He had promised their relatives that he would try to help them. And then he had risked his own freedom to keep those promises. In short, he had felt impelled to act beyond his own self-interest.

If goodness is simply equated with self-interest, then Terry Waite's explanation makes no sense. Apparent instances of goodness beyond self-interest must be dismissed. The cynic must insist that, despite all appearances, everything is in reality just self-interest. Even when the self-interest isn't obvious, it must still be there. More than that, it must be the only possible explanation of moral behaviour.

Now in the process, these cynical voices have actually paid a very heavy price. They have insisted that moral actions are not at all what they appear to be. They have insisted that the moral actors themselves are frauds or dupes. And they have insisted that they themselves alone have the correct explanation of moral behaviour. This explanation is, of course, self-interest. As human beings we only act out of self-interest ... short-term self-interest or long-term self-interest. We delude ourselves if we imagine reality is otherwise.

I suspect that most of us deep down know that this is moral nonsense. Even when we express ideas like this, we feel uneasy about them: they do not accord with our deepest sense of reality. For example, it is quite common to hear young people voicing such ideas when they first come to terms with the intricacies of evolutionary theory. They read a challenging book like Richard Dawkins's *The Blind Watchmaker*. They hear its message, that there is no design or purpose in the biological world – just the relentless pressure to survive. Then they quickly fall into the trap of seeing everything – not just the biological world, but the social and moral worlds as well – in its terms. For a while they hold that there is nothing beyond self-interest and the need to survive.

Then the doubts begin. There is obviously a great deal beyond self-interest and the need to survive. How could anyone think otherwise if they open their eyes to the moral behaviour of quite ordinary people? People caring for and loving cantankerous old people. It is easy to care for loving old people who constantly express gratitude. But the experience of many is that they go on caring long after gratitude has stopped. People in hospices caring for the terminally ill. People caring for the handicapped. People caring for the poorest of the poor. Even in a broken world, there is evidence all around us of goodness going beyond self-interest.

I suspect that this will become more obvious in the years to come. For much of the twentieth century religious faith has been in retreat. As the Chief Rabbi, Jonathan Sacks, argued so eloquently in his 1990 Reith Lectures: 'Twenty years ago it seemed as if religion had run its course in the modern world' (*The Persistence of Faith*, 1991, p. 94). Religious explanations of moral behaviour seemed to be thoroughly out of accord with reality. Props for the weaker-minded. Instead some remarkably thin explanations of moral behaviour took their place. Bertrand Russell, A.J. Ayer and others claimed at times that morality was based only on 'emotions' ... as if that was ever a sufficient basis even for their own deeply held moral convictions.

The moral philosopher A.E. Taylor was an important exception. He gave his Gifford Lectures at St Andrews in the late 1920s, at a moment in history not dissimilar to our own. Social and political ferment abounded. People were worried even then about Russia and about Europe. There was a severe economic depression, unemployment, and much cynicism. However, A.E. Taylor entitled his gentle and profound lectures 'The Faith of a Moralist'. One of the things that particularly attracts me about these lectures is that they took seriously the problem of goodness. Indeed, despite A.E. Taylor's love for Kant, he finally argued that morality and religious faith are intimately linked.

He expressed this powerfully in the following passage:

> The moral life itself, at its best, points to something which, because it transcends the separation of 'ought' from 'is', must be called definitely religion and not morality, as the source and inspiration of what is best in morality itself, and that the connection between practical good living and belief in God is much more direct and vital than Kant was willing to allow. I cannot doubt that morality may *exist* without religion. An atheist who has been taught not to steal or lie or fornicate or the like is, probably, no more nor less likely, in average situations, to earn his living honestly, to speak the truth, and to live cleanly, than a believer in God. But if the atheist is logical and in earnest with his profound view of the world, and the believer equally so with his, I think I know which of the two is the more likely to make irreparable and 'unmerited' grievous calamity a means to the purification and enrichment of personality (*The Faith of a Moralist*, 1932, vol. 1, pp. 155-6).

Of course, after more than sixty years, some of A.E. Taylor's language now seems antique. But his ideas are not. They were written from a deep concern to relate faith both to everyday life and also to the demands of reason. He was fully aware that many people who claim to lack faith effectively live as if they have faith. He was also aware that those who do claim to have faith do not always live up to this faith. Rather, what he argued was that there are good intellectual reasons for believing that morality makes better sense, when seen through the eyes of faith, than it does without this faith. He was patently aware of the scepticism of many of his fellow philosophers. Bertrand Russell was, after all, at the height of his powers then. But he was finally unconvinced by their purely secular accounts of moral behaviour.

For A.E. Taylor, goodness beyond self-interest (altruism if you wish) was both real and intellectually interesting. It pointed beyond. Indeed for him it pointed to a world created by a loving God ... something that 'transcends the separation of "ought" from "is" '. If the world really is created by a loving God, then the goodness beyond self-interest that we glimpse around us may well be a pointer to how things 'ought' to be. In moments of the 'is', particularly those moments which are less tainted by self-interest, we can glimpse the 'ought'. The creature can glimpse the intention of the Creator. None of this is possible for the atheist. The believer alone sets morality at this distinctive and, so Taylor believed, more profound, level of reality.

The problem of goodness beyond self-interest was also recognised by a few of the leading social scientists at the time. Outstanding among them must surely be R.H. Tawney. In their book *English Ethical Socialism* (1988), Norman Dennis and A.H. Halsey describe Tawney as 'the great modern master of ethical socialism: he offered the most complete expression of the tradition we seek to understand. In him the tradition reaches its highest point of personal accomplishment and its most comprehensive range of argument' (p. 2).

Dennis and Halsey both studied sociology under Tawney, at the London School of Economics, soon after the Second World War. Although they were undergraduates at the time, they came to know him as a human being as well as an intellectual. They clearly admired him at both levels. Tawney was the great intellectual champion of equality and had a profound effect upon many of the leaders of the Labour Party – as well as a number of Tories and Liberals. He was also an individual of great personal humility, who lived a very simple life-style (today we would surely call him a 'green'). When he entertained Archbishop William Temple to supper, he discussed politics and theology for hours and finally pulled out two plates of dried-up salad from behind the bookshelf!

In his early writings, Tawney showed that he was fully aware of the connection between ideas on equality and welfare and his own strong belief in a loving God. For him, it was precisely because he believed that we are all children of a loving God, that he also believed that we should treat each other equally and care for each other in moments of need. Yet as Britain became slowly more secular, so in later years Tawney tended to justify his moral and political ideas, in public at least, without much reference to religion. Did he lose his faith? His private journals tell quite a different story. He remained convinced that it was his religious faith which lay at the heart of his moral vision. Goodness beyond self-interest, and based in prayer, was crucial to his understanding of reality.

Tawney's legacy was not lost on the next generation of social thinkers in Britain. Norman Dennis and A.H. Halsey themselves are witnesses to this. There was also the remarkable study of altruism by Richard Titmuss, *The Gift Relationship* (1970). Titmuss noticed that quite ordinary people regularly act in ways that go beyond their immediate self-interest. The example that he took was blood donation. In Britain we give blood, we do not sell it. There is little or no reward for giving blood. It is, Titmuss argued, a small, but instructive, act of altruism.

There was also the influential study by Paul Halmos of the counselling world, which he entitled provocatively *The Faith of the Counsellors* (1965). It was a provocative title precisely because secular counsellors usually maintain that 'faith' has nothing to do with good counselling. It is a purely secular job. If clients want faith, they should go to a priest instead. In contrast, Halmos argued that at the heart of good counselling is a notion of 'care' which derives directly from the Christian idea of *agape* – or care beyond self-interest. Halmos's argument was all the more impressive because he did not claim to be a Christian himself.

What all these philosophers and social scientists were arguing, in their more personal moments of exploring reality, was that goodness, real goodness, raises problems for purely secular thought. Further, they argued this in an intellectual environment which was often self-consciously secular. If innocent suffering is a problem for those who believe in a loving God, then goodness beyond self-interest does appear to be a problem for those who do not.

Today, however, the intellectual environment seems to be changing. Jonathan Sacks added to the sentence just quoted about the apparent imminent demise of religion twenty years ago, the rejoinder: 'Today a more considered view would be that its story has hardly yet begun.' The last few years have witnessed extraordinary political changes. Ideological secularism is no longer the force it once was. With the collapse of the old Soviet Union, atheistic Marxism has few takers. The moral certainties that once characterised the Communist world, and which seemed so attractive to a previous generation of intellectuals, are in retreat. In addition, scientists today seldom claim – as many did a generation ago – that scientific knowledge is the only valid form of knowledge (in this respect Richard Dawkins is an exception). Most responsible scientists admit that their work is not value-free, and that the products of scientific technology can bring harm as well as good to the world. In short, scientists are faced with the claims of ethics. In the course of a generation, medical ethics, and now business ethics, have also become part of the serious agenda.

But if ideological secularism has retreated, secular liberalism lives on. It claims that there are no moral certainties – everything is changeable and nothing is fixed. Religious ideas are no longer to be attacked, but simply ignored. Morality is about not judging or harming others, it is not about anything positive. Live and let live. Pursue self-interest, but not to the harm of others.

Christian faith, I believe, says something far more challenging. It says, along with the faith of Jews and Muslims, and in deep contrast with secular liberalism, that there is an intimate connection between morality and faith. The way we view the universe has a direct connection with the way we should treat our neighbour. Loving God has everything to do with loving our neighbour, and loving our neighbour tells us much about whether we love God.

In the distinctively Christian story, this link is expressed graphically. Christianity presents a story about God loving us so much that he gave us his only Son. In Christ we believe that we can see God acting. In this good man we can see God. Goodness and Godness – so to speak – become fused; Christ as God's gift of love to us. So much so, that any good beyond self-interest that we may do, is not us, but Christ working through us. It is not we who are good; it is God who is good; and it is God in Christ working through us who is good.

Exploring reality through the eyes of faith is about vision. It is a vision sharply at odds with secular liberalism. 'Doing good' is not just about 'doing good' (after all, who wants to be a do-gooder), it is about doing the will of a loving God. At its deepest level, we seek to become more God-like in our lives. There is even a direct link here with prayer. In prayer we seek to listen … to seek the will of God … to learn how we should act as moral beings in the world that God has created in love. And finally, faith is about communities. Being a Christian, being a Jew, or being a Muslim, is about sharing together with others … sharing in worship and sharing in care. Worship and care, inextricably linked together, become our profoundest path to experiencing the Divine.

41

Professor Arthur Ellison

Let us consider first one or two facts about my fundamental approach, and a little basic epistemology. I am an applied scientist (an engineer) and not in the 'belief business'. My views about life and the universe are based on what I consider to be demonstrable facts, and reasonable deductions from them. And facts are no more and no less than the human experiences of normal people. As an open-minded student of psychical research I know well that paranormal experiences are quite common and not the sole perquisite of psychic people – it is just that they experience them rather more often than do the rest of us. Facts are interpreted ('understood', 'explained') in various ways in accordance with one's paradigms (mental models in terms of which we pattern and interpret our experiences) and our experiences are purely mental too. We have absolutely nothing else but mental experiences.

A mystical experience – an experience of the Divine – is most certainly paranormal. And every one of the world's great religions is, it seems clear, based on mystical experiences, interpreted by the founders in various ways, depending on their cultures. Paranormal experiences are often symbolic and expressed, in the case of the mystical experience, in archetypal form. They are certainly not experiences of the normal daily variety but much more deeply significant to those who have them.

Followers of all the religions, or of none, sometimes have mystical experiences. They realise that all life is one, that they are one with everything that exists, and at the heart of it all, the essence of everything, is the good, the true and the beautiful. Yet, in some paradoxical way, they are still themselves, while one with all other life. That, they say, is the most joyous and truly real experience they have ever had and they realise that everything is exactly as it is intended to be, moving towards some goal of perfection. Then the experience fades, and they are back to normality. Sometimes their lives are completely altered for the good by such an experience.

The near-death experience (NDE) is, it seems to me, if it goes sufficiently far, describable in some aspects as a mini-mystical experience. Since it has been discovered how to resuscitate a very recently clinically dead body, many millions of people, who would, in earlier times, have been pronounced dead, have had a near-death experience. At the stage of the NDE when the subject experiences what Moody calls in his book *Life After Life* the Being of Light, the subject, if he is a Christian, sometimes sees the traditional Christ of medieval paintings; if a Buddhist he may see the Buddha. A Jew would presumably sometimes see Abraham, a Muslim Mohammed. The figure is sometimes interpreted as God. It seems very clear that the experience is (to use the Jungian expression again) archetypal. Kenneth Ring suggests (in his own model) that the Being of Light is our own true Self. St Paul would perhaps have referred to that Being (in his model) as the Christ Within (one with the Father). A transpersonal psychologist would refer to it as the Self, a Theosophist as the Higher Self, at the Buddhic or Causal level of a human being.

However our experiences are interpreted – that is, whatever mental pattern we use (the results of our upbringing and the effects of our culture) – there is no doubt that experiences of the Being of Light and other even deeper and wider experiences of the Divine, are deeply significant and important and most certainly not the fantastic creations of a disorganised mind, the results perhaps of a lack of oxygen to the brain, or the side-effects of drugs. Those who suggest the latter are, in my view, sadly limited by their paradigm of a human being as an electrochemical machine. The evidence is conclusive that a model of a human being as merely an electrochemical machine is utterly inadequate to pattern all the mental experiences (and remember that we have nothing else) of a wide range of normal, healthy, rational human beings. However, it is a sad fact that our very wide range of useful cultural paradigms, commonplace (the physical world), scientific (sub-models of the physical world), or religious, are well-nigh impregnable for most people.

It is clear and easily understood why many people, especially those with the limited approach of so many scientists practising what Thomas Kuhn calls 'normal science' ('puzzle-solving within an unquestioned paradigm') dismiss too readily any human experiences that do not fit their paradigm. It is worth a little space to pursue this.

When a baby is born it surely has mental experiences – and they do not 'make sense'. Gradually, as a result of guided experiences and contact with its parents and others, it discovers that it is separate from a world around. The mental model we call the physical world (an object in which is our own physical body with its senses and brain and in terms of which we pattern those mental experiences) is established and reinforced along particular lines by parents and other authority figures. The schooling and perhaps further education of our Western culture reinforce and add detail to the big physical world paradigm. In our Western culture any experiences a child or young person may have which do not fit the paradigm are dismissed as fantasy, delusion or illusion – or in terms of the ever-useful and usually quite inappropriately applied word 'imagination'. As Thomas Kuhn explains, the paradigms of our culture (on which our language is based) decide for us what is possible and impossible, what is real or unreal, what is worth pursuing and what is not. (In a Western culture, for example, a parent would tell a child who had ostensible memories of a former incarnation that it had an over-active imagination. In the East it would probably be taken at its face value.)

Our paradigms are of great value to us. They enable us to 'understand' the experiences we have, to find our way around the 'physical world' (the overall big paradigm of our culture) and generally live our lives in a reasonably satisfactory and effective way. An 'explanation' of anything at all is merely a description in terms of some paradigm or other. Our paradigms are so valuable to us that the unconscious surrounds them with almost impregnable defensive bastions. These defences are especially strong for those normal scientists who have invested so much of themselves in the sub-paradigms of their scientific discipline, and which appear threatened by any evidence of the paranormal. (Anything which does not fit the normal cultural paradigms is called paranormal.) They fear, perhaps partly unconsciously, that their lives and careers will be threatened by such evidence. So their defences, when the evidence is good and therefore especially threatening, descend below reason and logic into anger and abuse, and ultimately into a rapid exit from the threatening facts. Every psychical researcher is familiar with this syndrome.

It is interesting to observe that other cultures have quite different paradigms. For example, the Hindu scholars refer to the normal physical world of us Westerners as a *maya* (Sanskrit for illusion) and say that things are not really as we believe. And certainly their paradigm, which is more like classical idealism, can lead to interesting mystical (spiritual) experiences, the results of *raja yoga* (meditation).

Perhaps, as the astronomer Sir James Jeans suggested, the universe really is 'more like a great thought than a great machine', and what we truly believe will become 'reality' for us. (Jung suggested something rather similar.) That would explain a great deal, in regard to religious belief and to some of the mysterious phenomena of psychical research, such as the Experimenter Effect and the Sheep/Goat Effect (where, respectively, the success of the same experiment with the same subjects depends on the experimenter and where the success depends on the prior beliefs of the subjects). It would also explain the occasional success of the child paranormal metal benders; would be an important basis of magic/witchcraft; and perhaps of psychic/spiritual healing.

But the mystical experience – the experience of the Divine – appears to be quite different from an experience of 'objects out there'. It must be worthwhile because it has been experienced by the noblest and finest members of the human race. One then has a consciousness above that of the levels of manifestation in terms of objects: it is at the levels of non-manifestation, of 'pure mind', pure creativity. That is, according to many traditions, the aim and object of manifestation and evolution. That is perhaps Moksha, Nirvana, where are to be found the 'pillars in the temple of thy God' who 'go out no more'. But, as an applied scientist, I perhaps speculate too much. There is no substitute for the facts of experience, that is, for trying and hopefully, in due time, seeing. And when we know we shall perhaps be quite unable to describe our experience because language necessitates an underlying agreed paradigm patterning a shared mental experience. Like the Buddha, we shall have to remain silent.

42

Ted Harrison

There are two kinds of journalist, the committed and the detached. Journalists reporting on religious affairs tend to be committed. They see their work as both an extension and an obligation of their faith. They write with enthusiasm to communicate the good news they have discovered. Journalists, however, who work for one of the grand institutions of the British media, are schooled in detachment. No Westminster correspondent is allowed to show his or her own political colours, and the industrial reporter must tread the middle way with care when unravelling and explaining the complexities of a labour dispute. I have spent nearly twenty years working as a journalist for BBC Radio, the British Independent Television Network and a number of the 'heavier' British newspapers. My background training is as a general news and current affairs reporter, but I have specialised in following and interpreting religious matters. It seemed to me, from early on in my career, that questions of faith were every bit as important as matters political and economic, in determining the course of events in the world; yet comparatively little attention was being paid to them by the secular media, even the grand institutions.

I determined from the start, however, to be detached rather than committed. I observed how other people claimed to be experiencing the Divine and how they reacted to what they believed God was expecting of them.

I developed the skills of the chameleon. Whatever the denomination, whatever the faith, of the worshippers around me I usually succeed in blending in with my surroundings. I have watched many moments of great spiritual intimacy, but have always felt it my role to stay mentally and emotionally detached, in order to observe and in order to report fairly and accurately on what I have seen.

I once sat in the dark in the monastery high up on the island of Patmos, the island of St John the Divine. The monks chanted their office as they and their forebears had done for a thousand years. Slowly, as my eyes became accustomed to the gloom, I became aware of the images and icons around me, blackened by the smoke of the many candles that had burned there over the centuries, but still discernible where the gold shone through. I could have allowed myself to feel as if I had been uplifted from the present and taken back in time. Instead I quietly turned on my tape recorder to capture the sound of the moment and inconspicuously made notes.

My response had been the same a few years earlier in Zambia when I witnessed a controversial African Roman Catholic Archbishop hold a mass service of exorcism. As people screamed, fainted and fought, I stayed in the background recording the evidence. It was pandemonium, a spiritual battlefield; yet my role, as I saw it, was to retain the cool head of the correspondent.

The media of mass communication are, by and large, most inappropriate channels when it comes to communicating aspects of the Divine. Deadlines are self-imposed time limits which are totally irrelevant to eternity. It was once said that trying to determine the course of history by reading the newspapers is like trying to tell the time by looking at the second hand of a watch. However, by and large, the means of mass communication are the only points of contact the vast majority of people have with the world of ideas.

As David Jenkins, the Bishop of Durham found, to use the mass media as a vehicle for theological debate is very unsatisfactory. When, on being appointed to his see, he opened up a familiar theological debate on the nature of the Virgin Birth and Resurrection to a wider public, it is unlikely that he expected to see such headlines as 'The fake miracles of Jesus, by a bishop' in the tabloid press. And yet, unless a person who sees his role as that of a Christian teacher is prepared to use the newspapers and television news to convey ideas, a number of important contemporary debates will spread no further than the walls of seminaries and be confined between the covers of academic textbooks. If all teachers refused to teach because they feared that every time they faced a class, some of those listening would misunderstand what they were saying, knowledge would never be passed on.

No newspaper article or broadcast programme, however good, can ever expect to convey a complete spiritual message or idea. God, or even any manifestation or reflection of the Divine, cannot be packaged into a neat 25-minute slot sandwiched between the television advertisements. The best a programme can hope to do initially, is trigger a response in a viewer which will set him or her off on a personal spiritual journey. Then what a work of journalism can also do is go some way towards validating an experience, which a viewer or reader has as a result of a personal journey of exploration. Through the window onto the outside world provided by the journalist an individual can be reassured that he or she is not alone: that there are others in the world seeking and finding what they interpret as experiences of the Divine and that there is no need to hide or feel ashamed of such experiences.

To give a highly unusual illustration of this from my own work, three years ago I met a man who had received the stigmata. He was not a man with any theological training or renowned for his piety. He was unemployed, living in a dark public-sector rented flat on the outskirts of one of Britain's major cities. He was understandably disturbed and worried by the bleeding from his hands. He had consulted his doctor, who in turn contacted me, having heard a radio programme I had compiled on the subject. I went to see his patient who was much relieved to know that his experience was not unique and that others, some of whom I had met and written about, were not dismissed as mad when they disclosed that they had the same marks and the same pain. He was particularly interested to learn that similar marks had been interpreted by others in the past as an experience given by God and that they had not been ridiculed for thinking that way.

So in a society where religious experience can lead to ridicule, the mass media can help authenticate that quest by being seen to take the subject seriously. And this can be seen when mainstream reporters and correspondents report on religious affairs and experience with the same detached but authoritative interest which correspondents in other fields bring to their own specialities.

The reporter on religious affairs cannot, however, authenticate individual claims. That would be like the arts correspondent siding with a critic. All that he or she can do is to say to believers and non-believers alike that the search for evidence of God at work in the world is a serious and valid one.

The impartial religious affairs correspondent is also an interpreter. Many groups of people with a valid spiritual insight to impart can only talk among themselves about that insight. Consequently religious cliques grow up, inward-looking and exclusive. Because no one understands their language of faith, they believe no one else has had their glimpse of the truth and they shut out the world to protect their 'secret'. And if their particular understanding of the truth demands that they evangelise, they will only accept new members on their own terms. Yet the mass media can give to members of these groups access to the thinking of others and a wider awareness of what all people on a spiritual quest have in common. Many members of exclusive groups do not want to be challenged by ideas from outside their protective shell of dogma and ritual, but do have, through radio, television and journals, the opportunity to discover that the search by people on this earth for an experience of the Divine, is a natural and universal facet of human behaviour.

Whether in the role of validator or interpreter, the religious affairs reporter needs to retain his or her impartiality in order to maintain authority and credibility. The personal search for a direct experience of the Divine has to be deferred.

43

The Rev. Don Cupitt

People are strikingly uncritical about their own religious experience. Almost without exception, they take it at face value, seeing it as in a mysterious manner giving them precious undistorted information from a source outside themselves. It is a sort of revelation, and people do not usually think of revelation as having been moulded by history and culture. Yet this assumption that religious experience is an innocent datum is hard to reconcile with the obvious fact that every religious experience turns out to be framed in the local vocabulary and to confirm some current local belief.

More than that, 'religious experience' itself has a history. The phrase was given its modern currency by William James, whose Gifford Lectures, *The Varieties of Religious Experience*, were published in 1902. *The Oxford English Dictionary* and its *Supplement* do not find any earlier use of the precise phrase 'religious experience'. But they remind us that the appeal to experience in religion is as old as British empiricism itself. It dates back at least to the late seventeenth century, to John Owen, and the heyday of puritan scholasticism.

Two points in puritan theology are vital to the understanding of why religious experience developed in our culture in the way it did. First, Calvin wanted Scripture alone to be the rule of faith, but was faced with the familiar problem of the diversity of interpretations. Did not this mean that there would always be the need for a powerful central teaching authority to control the interpretation of Scripture, as Rome claimed? Calvin replied that the prayerful and faithful reader of Scripture would be guided to interpret it aright by the inward testimony of the Holy Spirit. No Pope is needed, for God provides an inner way to Truth. Here, then, we see emerging already in Calvin himself a forerunner of the later Cartesian and Enlightenment belief that objective Truth can be determined within individual subjectivity.

The second way in which puritanism shaped our modern assumptions about religious experience was through its doctrines of irresistible Grace and Assurance. People were frantic for the assurance of salvation. If God's eternal decree is secret, how can I know that I am among the elect? Answer: I can be sure of final salvation if I have personally experienced the compelling power of Grace within my soul. God is almighty and does nothing in vain. If you have ever received Grace, then you may be certain of your own final salvation. And how can you be sure of having actually received it? By the sudden and irresistible force with which it rushes into the soul.

Thus puritanism could lead people to attach great importance to sudden, charismatic religious experiences, especially those which seem the most unmerited, unprepared-for and compulsive. Religious experience is like an orgasm from nowhere, warm and melting – and a very good thing to have, because it is a pledge of final salvation.

The subsequent history of religious experience in the Anglo-Saxon world has continued these themes. For example, if inner religious experience provides a short cut to Truth independent of the teaching authority of the Church, it is not surprising that to this day religious experience should remain so very common outside the churches (see David Hay, *Exploring Inner Space*, 1987, p. 130). Because of the puritan doctrines about election, irresistible Grace and assurance, people still want to view their own religious experiences as suddenly and purely given to them from Above. Because we have such a long tradition of bourgeois individualism and belief in empirical verification, we still to a quite remarkable degree assume that the objective Truth of momentous doctrines and theories can be decided just by events in our own personal psychological history. We Anglo-Saxons resisted Freud for so long because we didn't want to learn that the human mind is not a blank slate and is not by any means clean or innocent. On the contrary, Freud suggests, our subjective consciousness is only secondary, very incomplete, and all too often a profound falsification. We do not care for that, because we have been so Cartesian for so long. We have clung to our belief in the innocence of our religious experiences in the same way and for the same reasons as we have clung to our Cartesian notion of clear private consciousness and to our scientific empiricism.

We have believed in individual consciousness as the inner space wherein real Truth is given to us and tested by us. We have felt confident that we can tell which of the psychic events cropping up in our souls has no natural cause and therefore must have been sent from Above. Freud or no Freud, these convictions have proved singularly durable.

They have, however, become overlaid by later developments. The two main superimposed strata might be called Methodist and Romantic. The Methodists linked puritanism with today's Evangelical, Pentecostal and Charismatic movements. The Romantics, and especially figures such as Wordsworth and Emerson, took religious experience out of the fellowship meeting and the chapel and made it natural. It became something like a mode of response to an unbounded whole of which one felt oneself to be a part, a response that was both intuitive and reconciling. Religious experience was aestheticised, but it remained in some sense informative, and people still see it as somehow warranting an optimistic view of life and the world.

This historical background, I submit, explains the way religious experience is handled in the work of modern apologists such as Sir Alistair Hardy and David Hay. In their surveys they have posed questions like: 'Have you ever been aware of or influenced by a presence or power, whether you call it God or not, which is different from your everyday self?' Alternatively: 'Have you ever felt as though you were very close to a powerful spiritual force that seemed to lift you out of yourself?' Over the past thirty years, in Britain and the USA, about a third of the population have been answering Yes to these questions (Hay, pp. 120-34), and I am arguing that the way the questions are framed and answered, and the way the answers are interpreted, is all to be explained against the historical background I have sketched. Our religious experiences are the product of our own particular cultural and intellectual history. Figures like Calvin and Descartes, Jonathan Edwards and John Wesley, Wordsworth and William James, gave us philosophical assumptions to which we still cling, instructed us that religious experiences were desirable, and prescribed the form that they must take – and, indeed, do take. Among us, at least. If we were Tibetans, our assumptions would be very different. But here and with this history behind us, we see things as we do, and take our way of seeing them for granted.

I hope I have now explained a paradox. People in our tradition assume that their own religious experiences are *not* historically conditioned, but are clean natural data given to them from Above. I have outlined an historical explanation of why they are systematically unaware of the historicality of their own religious experiences.

I don't mean to sound sceptical. I am no sceptic. But I am saying that historicising religious experience is the only way to make it intelligible. How else could we hope to explain the fact that every religious-experience report is as much tied to a particular cultural context as any other kind of writing? People's religious experiences invariably reflect locally-held beliefs. As Hume said in connection with miracles, the religious experiences of different religions would all cancel each other out, unless we can learn to see each religion as producing its own tradition of experience internally. Your religious experience is an *expression* of your local religious tradition, and not a piece of independent evidence for its truth.

The local religious background also makes the logic of religious experience intelligible. After all, the David Hay questions are very perplexing in terms of classical Christianity, which regarded God as unknowable. From patristic times God was infinite and simple, altogether transcending the categories through which the human mind might understand him. Nowadays, though, pollsters and respondents appear to share the assumption that some sort of knowledge-by-experience of God is possible. They even seem to suppose that there is a valid inference from 'I am in a certain psychological state', to 'I am experiencing none other than *God*'. How is this possible? The history I have sketched gives the answer. The puritans fully accepted that God cannot be known directly, but in their theology the scripture-guided believer was justified in referring certain special states of the soul to God as their cause. This means that in their own way the puritans also set religious experience within an interpretative context. It is not clean or natural. It arises within a specific faith-community. Scripture forms it, and helps us to interpret it.

I'm saying something rather similar. The student of religion must explain religious experience purely immanently, that is, historically. Your religious experience is your religious and cultural tradition expressing itself through you and in your life-experience. Catholics have Catholic experiences, Protestants have Protestant experiences. Even within the Hebrew Bible it is already being said that the criterion of authenticity for a prophecy or vision is its conformity with the orthodox tradition that produced it and that it must reflect and confirm (e.g. Deuteronomy 13:1, 18:15-20). My culturalism or expressivism explains why conformity with the local orthodoxy has to be the criterion of genuineness. There cannot *be* any other criterion.

Very well. But suppose you accept all this: suppose you join me in seeking to become a fully-demythologised believer of the new post-realist kind. Can people like us still enjoy the consolations of religious experience? Yes, we can. It is true that we have given up the illusions of supernaturalism, and therefore have lost that sudden, compelling, given-from-outside quality. Our religion has become a continuous and fully-immanent movement of signs. There is still innovation, but we know nothing of any violent irruption from outside. The world of signs is outsideless. Nevertheless, our religion can still be aesthetically beautiful, creative and joyous. After Truth, our religious experience coincides with our religious *activity*.